A
SHORT
GUIDE
TO

# GOSPEL
# GENEROSITY

A SHORT GUIDE TO

# GOSPEL GENEROSITY

## Giving as an Act of Grace

### NATHAN W. HARRIS

**B&H**
PUBLISHING
BRENTWOOD, TENNESSEE

To Noah and Jude:

I pray that you both come to know, love, and serve
the Lord Jesus Christ for all of your lives. May the gospel
take hold of you and lead you to a life of generosity—to
serve others and glorify God.

*For you know the grace of our Lord Jesus Christ:*
*Though he was rich, for your sake he became poor,*
*so that by his poverty you might become rich.*
—2 Corinthians 8:9

# Acknowledgments

A BOOK IS NEVER written by just one person. Throughout the process of writing, authors are influenced, encouraged, and challenged by a multitude of people in a variety of ways. The reality is this; writing does not take place in a vacuum but progresses by a symphony of fellowships. I am grateful for the mentors, friends, colleagues, and family who have been my idea sparing partners, prayerful support, and encouragement along the way. I would be remiss to not acknowledge your impact on my life and writing. Because the truth is, without many of you, this book project would have never come to fruition.

For years my mentors and friends had to suffer through numerous conversations on my love for Greek conjunctions, the letter to the Hebrews, and how the gospel impacts generosity. Without each of you, I would have never been challenged and encouraged to pursue writing on gospel generosity. The

Lord has been kind to give me close fellowship with each of you: Charles Smith Jr., Jared Bumpers, Eric Turner, Jason Kees, Todd Chipman, Mike Brooks, Ronni Kurtz, Brandon Smith, and Stephen Weingart. To say I am grateful for each of you is an understatement. To my colleagues at Grace College & Seminary, you had the pleasure (more like displeasure!) of hearing me talk about gospel generosity daily. To the Grace advancement team, you listened as I developed my thoughts out loud, you asked questions that made me rethink my writing, and you prayed for me as I sprinted to the finish line. Each of you played an integral role in the writing process, and I can't thank you enough! Particularly, I want to thank my president and friend, Dr. Drew Flamm, for his consummate support from start to finish. I also want to express my gratitude to my editor, Mary Wiley, and the team at B&H Publishing. Thank you for taking a chance on me and giving me the space to write on generosity.

To my family, what can I say? Mom and Dad, you have always encouraged me to pursue what the Lord has called me to do. Thank you for cheering me on and modeling a life of generosity. Billy and Marissa, it is one thing to be close to your siblings, but it is another to consider them dear friends.

I am beyond grateful for your love and friendship! Tim and Lynne, I have not only been blessed with incredible parents, but also with incredible in-laws. Thank you for loving me as your own and supporting me in my calling. Kelsey, Noah, and Jude, even as I type this acknowledgment for you, I am smiling because of the great joy you each bring me. Your patience, love, encouragement, and occasional writing accountability are the reasons I was able to write *A Short Guide to Gospel Generosity*. I love you more than you know!

Last and certainly not least, none of this would be even possible without the Lord's kindness and grace in my life. I thank the Lord for His love and mercy, each and every day. I pray gospel generosity not only spurs on believers to see how their giving is transformed by the gospel, but that it honors and glorifies Jesus Christ in every way.

# Contents

# CHAPTER 1

# What Is Gospel Generosity?

*For you know the grace of our Lord Jesus Christ:*
*Though he was rich, for your sake he became poor,*
*so that by his poverty you might become rich.*
—2 Corinthians 8:9

MONEY. IT'S EVERYWHERE. WELL, not literally, but it is easy to see how that figurative language isn't exactly hyperbole. Money may not be falling all around us, growing from a tree, or being handed out freely, but we think about it every day. We work absurd schedules to make more of it, we save it for our futures and our families, and we often spend it quicker than it appears. If money isn't already on the forefront of your mind, then let our culture remind you about it on a daily basis. It's impossible to escape hearing about money when we turn on

1

the TV, watch movies, or even listen to music. Every news station nationwide can quickly alter your mood, and the rest of its viewers, by informing us about the current state of the stock market or bemoaning the rising cost of living. Movies have been written, directed, and produced to exhibit the seemingly glorious life of wealth and the benefits of money. And no matter the genre, musicians for decades have focused on money as the main theme for one's life. In many ways, with a focus on accruing wealth, it seems like we are all living as if life is "all about the Benjamins." The world tells us, "The more money you have, the happier you will be!" By culture defining success and happiness as the life for the one who has means, we've lost all awareness of what it means to give instead of receive. Our focus has become purely on accumulating and displaying our wealth, instead of stewarding and giving what we have. Money is now a means to happiness, and not a means for radical generosity.

But culture isn't the only thing to blame for how we save and spend our money while neglecting to give generously. Even within certain Christian circles, we have heard for years that we must be good stewards of our money; therefore, we must save every penny we have. Under this teaching, the

Christian's highest aim for money is to save at all costs, which includes eating rice and beans for every dinner. Why? All for the sake of saving money and to give a Christian a sense of financial peace. While I say that somewhat tongue in cheek, I don't disagree with the notion of being good financial stewards. But for a Christian to be a financial steward of his or her money without living a life of radical generosity is like being a musician without an instrument or a pilot without a plane. In either of those cases, you are missing a very important part of who you are and how you live your life. As Christians, you can't be stewards of your finances without living out your call to generosity. The issue with focusing so much on saving money is that it often makes us believe that financial peace only comes through money. We tend to trust in our ability to save, and not the sufficiency of God to provide. Ultimately, in fear of losing our newfound financial peace, we ignore the Christian's call to give. We are told to "save, save, save," but the gospel calls us to "give, give, give."

Surely, there is more to life than just gaining and saving money, right? I answer that question with a hearty, yes! This book is all about one thing—giving. More specifically, it's about how the gospel calls Christians to a life of radical generosity. But let me ask, why do we struggle with giving so much? I think the answer is twofold: first, as Christians, we often think that when we give our lives to Christ, He takes hold of everything except our money. Therefore, we don't recognize how we are stewards of God's resources, which are to be used for God's purposes. And second, because we don't like to talk about money, we don't have a proper biblical foundation for thinking about giving. First, let's address the former because it impacts the latter.

## A BAPTIZED POCKETBOOK

As Christians, we know that God has freely given to us. He has given to us His grace, patience, kindness, love, blessing, etc., and most importantly, He has given His very own Son to redeem us, and His Spirit to seal us (Eph. 1:1–14). And yet, though God has freely given, and has modeled generosity throughout all of redemptive history, generosity and giving seem to be the last things on our minds as Christians. For centuries theologians have believed there are three conversions a person must experience: the conversion of the head, the conversion of the heart, and the conversion of the pocketbook.[1]

We can agree with many before us, the conversion of the pocketbook is most difficult. Now, that's not to say your money and finances will eventually come to the saving knowledge of Jesus Christ, but it does means that after you become a Christian, your thinking and affections are transformed, and the way you view your money is different. Though your pocketbook doesn't get saved, you do; and therefore, how you view your money is transformed. Regardless of who said that quote, the sentiment of it rings true. It's like we hear the gospel, respond in faith, and yet hold our money in tight fists away from the Lord. But through the Holy Spirit's work of sanctification, not only are our heads and hearts transformed by the gospel, but every single aspect of our lives receives conversion—including our bank accounts.

If you love history, or are from Texas, chances are that you know the name Sam Houston. One could hardly say that Sam had an easy life and picturesque upbringing, nor was he the prime example of moral uprightness. Born in Virginia in 1793, Sam moved to Tennessee with his mother and eight siblings after his father passed away. In 1809 Sam ran away and spent three years living with the Cherokee in Tennessee, where he adopted many of their customs and learned their language. In

1812, Houston joined the U.S. Army to fight against Britain in the War of 1812. It was during that war that Houston suffered three nearly fatal wounds that he dealt with for the rest of his life. By gaining favor with Andrew Jackson, Houston worked his way through the political ranks, receiving local, state, and national recognition. Houston spent the entirety of his life fighting wars, battles, and leading in revolution.

Throughout the majority of his life, Houston would not have been known for being kind, gentle, or generous. But what makes Houston's story remarkable is not his military or political career, but his conversion. Through Lyndon Johnson's great-grandfather, George Washington Baines Sr., Houston heard the gospel of Jesus Christ and became a Christian within years of his death. After his conversion, Houston was a changed man. No longer belligerent and tough, Houston's newfound life was marked by peace and contentment. On the day that Houston was to be baptized, people came from far and wide to witness such an occasion. I imagine it is because many knew what Houston was like and wanted to be eyewitnesses of his baptism. And like many historical stories, lore has handed down to us an interesting story about an interaction between Houston and the pastor as he was getting baptized. As he walked down to the river's edge, the pastor saw that Houston still had his watch on his hip. Quickly pointing it out to Houston, the man took it off and handed it to a friend. The pastor then remarked, "You'd better hand him your wallet too," but Houston simply responded, "No, I believe not, pastor. I'm afraid it needs baptizing too."[2] From that day forward, Houston's baptism marked a changed life. Not only did he experience new life in Christ, but he became a staunch supporter for the cause of Christ. Not only was his life converted, but so was his pocketbook. He used his wealth to support Christian ministries, Christian colleges, and even paid for half of his pastor's annual salary until his death. Houston now knew that living as a Christian meant walking in generosity. His baptism marked for him a baptism of his whole life. His pocketbook became immersed, quite literally, to be used for the kingdom of God. For Houston nothing, including his money, was to be kept from God's cause.

Sam Houston is a great example of what it means for the head, heart, and pocketbook to be converted. When a person is converted to Christ, it's not just one part of his life that is transformed while the other aspects remain the same. No, the entirety of his life is converted. Not one piece of someone's life is left out of that conversion. After putting faith in the atoning work of Jesus, your entire life is used for the glory of God. All things, yes, all things including your money, are used for God's glory. As the head is converted, its focus is to think of the things of God. As the heart is converted, its affections and desires grow for the things of God. Because your head and heart are converted, then even how you view your money changes. What once used to be yours is now for God's use. As the pocketbook experiences conversion, its aim is to be used to glorify God. A converted life leads to converted thinking about money. A converted pocketbook does not heed the words of the world and fixate itself on saving, but sees its resources as a way to participate in the gospel's call to generosity. The call to follow Christ means to commit your whole life without reservation or hesitation. Every aspect of your life is given sacrificially to God, which includes your money. Because of God's mercy, and the new life we find in Christ, Christians should live out their holy call to generosity with joy.

The apostle Paul never falls short of telling believers how to live in light of their new-found faith in Christ. Working through one of the most notoriously difficult sections in

Scripture (Romans 9–11), Paul tells the church about the mystery of Israel, salvation, and God's mercy. Paul then says,

> Therefore, brothers and sisters, in view of the mercies of God, I urge you to present your bodies as a living sacrifice, holy and pleasing to God; this is your true worship. Do not be conformed to this age, but be transformed by the renewing of your mind, so that you may discern what is the good, pleasing, and perfect will of God. (Rom. 12:1–2)

We don't have the time or space in this book to do an exegetical deep dive down to the bottom of this passage, but at first blush three things stick out immediately to us. First, we see that the foundation for how Christians should live is based upon the great mercy of God. Second, Paul calls the Christian life a living sacrifice. And third, the life of a Christian must be antithetical to the ways of the world. Let's briefly think about each of these points and how Paul pleads with the Roman church to seek and serve God by giving the whole of their lives. Let's focus on that second point: living for God means living sacrificially in all aspects of our lives.

As I've said for years, if you want to understand the New Testament better, you must first understand the Old Testament. There are so many Old Testament passages quoted, echoed, and alluded to throughout the entire New Testament, pointing believers to Christ and how the Christian is to walk in newness of life. But we often miss the beauty and nuance of a New Testament passage when we don't grasp its Old Testament underpinnings. Romans 12:1–2 is not exempt from this general rule.

I cannot overstate the difficulty of Romans 9–11, even Paul calls it a mystery (11:25)! But regardless of how one interprets this passage with regard to Israel and salvation, the common thread through all of it is God's mercy. Paul moves from chapters 9–11 in order to call Christians to live according to what he has just said, and he begins with a "therefore" statement. I love when we encounter a "therefore" when reading the Bible. As someone who has geeked out on conjunctions during much of his doctoral work, I find these little words to be packed with theological importance. Not only do they help us read a passage as connected together, but they tell us how the passage should be read as well. The old cliché still remains a helpful tool for us to use when reading; so we must ask ourselves: "What is the therefore there for?" You should read a "therefore" like a big red stop sign in the text. Just as a stop sign makes you stop and look, so does the "therefore" in Romans 12. We stop when we see "therefore," and we look around. Paul purposefully intends for his readers, including us, to read therefore and first look backward before we read ahead. Everything that Paul has said before is the foundation and setup for what is to come.

If he were simply to command the Roman church to be "living sacrifices" without the preceding context, many would ask: "Why?" But because Paul points them backward, the church hears the reason for holy living—God's mercy. You don't understand the importance of Paul's call to live as a sacrifice without understanding how God's mercy has impacted you. It's because of God's mercy that the believer experiences redemption and salvation in Jesus Christ. God's mercy is the foundational motivator for the Christian life. We live sacrificially, as Paul says, because we've experienced God's kindness, love, and mercy found only in the sacrifice of His Son, Jesus Christ.

It's no wonder that Paul calls on Christians to be a "living sacrifice." Yet sometimes this command is lost on twenty-first-century Christians. In order to illustrate how Christians are to respond to the mercy of God, Paul uses the sacrificial practices of Israel as the perfect example, showing us how we are to live until Christ returns. He reminds them that because of God's great mercy, Christians are called to live differently. What does this look like in our lives? Paul compares our lives to that of a living sacrifice presented to God, which is holy and pleasing. Don't skip over that line too quickly or you will miss a theological truth Paul intended for believers of all time to hear. He uses an oxymoron, "living sacrifice." Sacrifices aren't living; in fact, that is the opposite of a sacrifice.

Throughout the Old Testament, especially in Leviticus, we find the intended outcome of sacrifice—death. Animals' lives were regularly sacrificed to provide atonement for the sins of God's people. Without death, sacrifice was not achieved. What was once alive, now no longer lived because it had been sacrificed for the glory of God and the cleansing of His people. Not one part of that animal was excluded in the sacrificial process. Through sacrifice, animals weren't partially killed and left to survive. Or, to quote my favorite movie, *The Princess Bride*, animals weren't "mostly dead" after they were sacrificed. They were totally and utterly dead. Sacrifice meant death, and the entirety of the animal's life was given up to God. This is exactly how Paul says Christians are to respond to God's mercy, to live sacrificially, by giving over their whole life to God. Their life is to be handed over as a sacrifice, to be totally and utterly devoted daily to pursuing holy living, which is pleasing to God. Christians, as living sacrifices, are to give over every aspect of their lives to God. They put to death their old ways and live sacrificially. As a living sacrifice, the Christian life is intended to be entirely dedicated to God's call and cause. There is nothing in the Christian life that is kept separate from a relationship to God. You can't be a living sacrifice while keeping certain aspects of your life, like your money, separated from God. Ultimately, God's mercy drives Christians to be living sacrifices, not being conformed to the things of this age, but transformed to be focused on the things of God. To be a living sacrifice means to forsake the ways of this world and to serve the living God. A living sacrifice is utterly and totally "all in" for God's call and cause for the Christian's life.

Sam Houston is a prime example of what it looks like for someone to live sacrificially in all aspects of life. As he came to faith and was baptized, he did not see how he could keep his money away from God's use. Through faith in Christ, every part of Houston's life had been changed, and the picture of baptism symbolizes the cleansing of one's whole life. It wasn't just the head and heart of Houston that were changed by the gospel, but his pocketbook was changed too. Houston saw fit to sacrificially give as a way to proclaim his new life in Christ. As a Christian, has your pocketbook experienced a baptism of sorts? Has God's mercy driven you to be a living sacrifice in all areas of your life? Another way to ask that is, have you committed everything in your life, including your bank account, to be used for God's glory and His kingdom?

As we have seen in Romans 12:1–2, because of God's mercy, the call for Christians is to live sacrificially. Every aspect of their lives is given over to God, for His purpose and for His glory. This includes not only how we view and spend our money, but how we live generously with all of the time, resources, and gifts God has given us too. Just as God's mercy is the foundation for our new living, the gospel is the foundation for how we are to give as well.

## WHAT IS GOSPEL GENEROSITY?

I can't think of many conversations that can cause as much of a controversy with your family at the dinner table, or during a holiday, as a discussion on money. Except for maybe politics! It's not just the topic of money that causes strife and disagreement within your family; it's telling people what they should do with their money. Whether your family members are giving unsolicited advice on investments or sharing with you their opinions on savings, spending, and giving, no one wants to talk about it. We want to make those decisions on our own because our money is, well, ours. We typically shut them out, pretend to listen, or find an excuse to leave the room. We don't like talking about it openly because money is a deeply personal issue for many of us.

Unfortunately, this happens within our church families as well. The moment a pastor begins to talk about giving, taking up the offering, or capital projects, you can hear the collective sound of wallets being clenched and the grip on purses tightening. And often, church goers are tempted to think, *Here we go again; they just want more money.* Now I know this is somewhat a caricature of our churches in the United

States of America, but I challenge you to talk to your pastor and ask how much pushback he receives when preaching on giving and generosity. I think you may be surprised! Because money is a deeply personal and intimate topic for many of us, which we will address in the next chapter, we find a myriad of responses when discussing it within the church. Preaching on giving is either met with exuberate affirmation or extreme opposition, and there isn't often an in-between.

What causes this phenomenon? Why are people so averse to hearing about the Christian call to give? Just as we need to be reminded that God's mercy drives us to live sacrificially (Rom. 12:1–2), we need to be reminded that the gospel is the foundation for how we live generously (2 Cor. 8:9). Just as God's mercy drives us to live a life wholly devoted to Him, it's the divine exchange we find in the gospel that motivates our radical generosity.

Often when preaching or teaching on giving, pastors and church staffs find themselves going immediately to 2 Corinthians 8–9. For good reasons, those few chapters are a great guide when discussing the need for generosity. The apostle Paul approaches the Corinthian church with many needs and shares of how other local churches are giving in order to advance God's mission on the earth. Frankly, it's a beautiful depiction of how God's people live in light of the gospel and give generously.

In those two chapters, we find many ways the apostle Paul teaches the idea of generosity, calling the Corinthian church to give. By using another local church as an example, he tells how God's grace manifested in the life of the Macedonian church as radical generosity. Though the Macedonian church was experiencing "a severe trial brought about by affliction," it was the "grace of God . . . given to the churches" that enabled them to have "abundant joy" and show how "their extreme poverty overflowed in a wealth of generosity on their part" (2 Cor. 8:1–2). Because of the grace of God, the Macedonians didn't let something like poverty stop them from exhibiting the wealth they have in God and give to those in need. In fact, Paul even says that those within the Macedonian church "begged us earnestly for the privilege of sharing in the ministry to the saints" (2 Cor. 8:4). Have you ever noticed that verse when reading through the passage before? The Macedonian church "begged" to participate in the "privilege" of giving. Giving for them wasn't an obligation or option; it was a privilege that they earnestly desired to participate in.

Their eagerness and willingness to join in the privilege of giving showed up in how they gave, or perhaps should we say, "how much" they gave. By God's grace, their abundant joy overflowed into generosity by not only giving "according to their ability" but "even beyond their ability" (2 Cor. 8:3). The Macedonian church, fueled by God's grace, genuinely desired to give generously despite living in the reality of poverty. For Pau, and the Macedonian church, giving is not predicated upon a surplus of wealth but upon generous hearts affected by the grace of God. What we find in these few verses is the simple fact: you don't have to be wealthy to give, but radical generosity is shown by those with abundant joy and a genuine eagerness to participate in the Lord's work. By the world's standards, the Macedonian church was poor, but according to God's grace, they were wealthy in generosity.

By highlighting the generosity of the Macedonian church, Paul calls the Corinthian church, and us too, to excel in the very same act of grace. As Christians are to excel in "everything—in faith, speech, knowledge, and in all diligence, and in your love for us," Paul also calls for the church to "excel also in this act of grace" (2 Cor. 8:7). Just as much as Christians are to grow in things like faith, speech, knowledge, diligence, love, and so forth, we are also to grow in the act of generosity. Generosity is not a second-rate characteristic or practice for the believer. We are to excel in it just as we are to grow in our faith, speech, knowledge, diligence, and love. That means that generosity is not a work obligated for the believer but is a result of God's grace. Just as God's grace matures believers in their faith, seasons their speech, deepens their knowledge, disciplines them to diligence, and enlarges their affections in love, they also grow in their eagerness to be generous givers—all by God's grace. I think this is why Paul ultimately says, "I am not saying this as a command" (2 Cor. 8:8) when he encourages them to grow in their generosity, because giving is not a legal requirement but a joyful participation in God's work.

One of my earliest memories attending church as a young boy was watching the offering plate being passed along between the pews. Week in and week out I saw that offering plate go from one side of the church to the other, and the whole time, church members were dropping envelopes or cash in the plate. Each week as the plate reached my family, I would see my dad take out our envelope with a check and drop it into the offering plate. After a few weeks of watching him do that, I remember asking him: "Why do you have to give money at church every week?" And I will never forget my dad's response: "I don't have to give; I *get* to give." My parents saw their weekly giving not as an obligation to the church but an opportunity to participate in its ministry. Giving wasn't a burden but a joy for them to live generously. Those that are affected by the goodness of God's grace joyfully give, knowing that it's a privilege. Christians should not ask themselves, "Do I have to give?" but when they encounter God's grace in their lives, they can't help but give. Abundant joy in God's grace leads to a wealth of generosity—no matter your financial situation.

If the Corinthian church were not convinced of Paul's persuasive discussion on giving, he hammered the nail on the head by explaining how the gospel shapes generosity. In 2 Corinthians 8:9 Paul reminds the Corinthian church that generosity is rooted in the gospel. Yes, it's God's grace that enables believers to grow in faith, love, and generosity, but it's the gospel that is the foundation for the transformation of your head, heart, and pocketbook. To support his call to generosity and giving, the apostle Paul takes the Corinthian church straight to the gospel. It's there where the believer finds their basis for giving and their foundation for radical generosity. For it's in the gospel, and only the gospel, that Christians can see giving as a privilege and generosity as a joy. Here's what Paul says by the inspiration of the Holy Spirit: "For you know the grace of our Lord Jesus Christ: Though he was rich, for your sake he became poor, so that by his poverty you might become rich" (2 Cor. 8:9). Paul reminds them, and us, that the gospel is a divine exchange; Christ became poor so that in Him we experience the fullness of His riches. It's in this simple statement Christians begin to desire to live generously, because Christ gave to us generously. It was for our sake Christ gave up his riches to become poor, so that through his poverty we then become rich.

This isn't the only time Paul shows the Corinthian church how the divine exchange in the gospel provides believers with Christ's benefits. Paul points the Corinthians to the gospel as the foundation for their reconciliation. Paul explains, "He made the one who did not know sin to be sin for us, so that in him we might become the righteousness of God" (2 Cor. 5:21). Though Christ did not know sin, He became sin so that we could be reconciled to God. By Christ taking on our sin, we then take on His righteousness and stand before God as those who have been justified. Just as Christ did not know sin but became sin, He also gave up His riches to become poor for our benefit. It's through the gospel Christians experience the richness of Jesus Christ. This isn't to say that through the gospel we all become millionaires; no, it means that we are saved through Christ humbling Himself to die on the cross (Phil. 2:8). The gospel is our foundation for generosity because it tells us that we can give because Christ has first given to us. Though we were once poor ourselves, we now experience the richness of Christ, which overflows as a wealth of generosity. Generosity is rooted in the gospel, sprouts from the gospel, and bears fruit because of the gospel. Giving is not merely a virtue for the Christian life; it is a cheerful disposition that springs forth from the good news of salvation in Jesus Christ. This is why the Macedonian church had an abundance of joy even though they faced severe trials and afflictions, because they knew where their hope was—in the work of Christ! Generosity is a fruit of the gospel that arises from new life in Christ, is empowered by the Holy Spirit, and has been modeled by the Father throughout all of creation. It is a sign of the radical reforming of the believer's head and heart to joyfully serve the Lord through the stewardship of their resources. Thus, generosity for the Christian is not just about giving, but also about proclaiming and portraying the saving work of God. For every Christian, the divine exchange found in the gospel is the foundation for a life of generous giving. The call to Christ is a life called to generosity—sharing one's own time, talent, and treasure for the kingdom of God.

Therefore, gospel generosity is simply giving that is rooted in the saving work of Jesus Christ. It is the Christians' joyful awareness of what Christ has done for them and how they are privileged to participate in proclaiming that work through giving and advancing the gospel.

## ANSWERING THE CALL TO GOSPEL GENEROSITY

At the beginning of this opening chapter, I said that our issue with money and giving is twofold: first, as Christians, we often think that when we give our lives to Christ, He takes hold of everything except our money. Therefore, we don't recognize how we are stewards of God's resources, which are to be used for God's purposes. And two, because we don't like to talk about money, we don't have a proper biblical foundation for thinking about giving. The first was answered by showing that when God calls us to faith in Christ, the entirety of our lives is given over to God. Not one aspect of us is left outside of God's sovereignty. As we are baptized, every part of us, including our pocketbooks, is cleansed and finds transformation in the gospel. As a living sacrifice, the Christian's aim is to live a holy and devoted life before the Lord. The second issue finds its resolution in knowing that the gospel is our foundation for generosity. In the gospel believers find their joy in giving and, no matter their financial status, exhibit wealth in Christ.

If generosity finds its foundation in the gospel and is to be lived out by Christians in their daily lives, then we must take seriously the call to give. We cannot seek to grow and excel in faith, love, and knowledge while neglecting the act of grace known as giving. We need to embrace the reality that as believers, giving is not a legal requirement or optional practice, but a privilege to participate in gospel ministry.

How do we embrace a life of gospel generosity? The first thing to do is, well, give. I know that seems incredibly reductionistic and silly to say, but it is often the hardest step for Christians to take. So, if you want to practice generosity, the best thing you can do is make giving a habit in your life. Beyond simply giving, let me encourage you to seek a biblical and theological framework for what it means for Christians to live lives of joyous generosity. To do that, we must look to the Word of God, that is profitable for all areas of our lives and equips us for every good work (2 Tim. 3:16–17). So, as you begin contemplating what generosity looks like for you, let me invite you to join me through the rest of this book as we begin to answer some of life's biggest questions concerning generosity and giving. Let's explore the Bible together as we seek to excel in this act of grace—generosity.

## WHERE ARE WE GOING?

I am not that old, but when I was younger, we didn't have GPS in our phone—let alone in our car! When we took a road trip, we had to map out exactly where we were going before we left our house. Looking at a map and understanding exactly where you are going before you begin your trip helps you get safely (and timely) to your destination. Therefore, it is equally important for us to lay out a "road map" before going much further. This will ensure that we aren't aimlessly wandering around the topic of giving but are moving in the direction of understanding how the gospel fuels our generosity.

Throughout the rest of this book, each of the chapters will cover a topic that will help us consider how Christians should understand their call to gospel generosity.

Over the next few chapters, we will discuss:

1. How our obsession with money and possessions is an issue of heart, health, and service to God.
2. How the Christian is no longer bound to Old Testament tithing.
3. How Jesus transforms giving in the New Testament.
4. How giving can proclaim and portray the gospel to the world around us.
5. How we are to give in anticipation of Christ's return.

## DISCUSS

1. We believe that 2 Timothy 3:16 is true. Scripture is not just "inspired" by God but is also useful in teaching and training us in all areas of our lives. But have you ever considered that

you may be letting culture and society impact your views on money and giving more than God's Word? What are some practical ways you can begin to make a course correction on what influences you most?

2. The story of Sam Houston is remarkable. Someone as tough and cruel as he was experienced an incredible life change because of the gospel of Jesus Christ. When you came to faith in Christ, did you give over everything to God? Another way to ask is: Have your pocketbook and bank account been kept separate from God, or did it get baptized too?

3. How has the conversion of your head and heart influenced the way you give money to your local church, missionaries, ministries, the needy, and so forth?

4. What are you hoping to learn the most by studying a biblical and theological understanding of generosity and giving? Beyond gaining knowledge, how do you plan to implement what you learn through this book?

## CHAPTER 2

# Our Obsession with Possessions

*"You cannot serve both God and money."*
—Matthew 6:24

HOW DID WE BECOME so obsessed with money? It is not a new issue in the twenty-first century but has been around from the beginning of time.[1] In fact, an unhealthy obsession with money and possessions isn't a foreign topic to the Bible either. From Genesis to Revelation, we have seen how a poorly guided desire for possessions has been at the epicenter of numerous biblical accounts. Whether God's people did not provide a worthy offering (Gen. 4:3–5), took offerings that did not belong to them (1 Sam. 2:17), rejected the Lord's blessing by robbing Him (Mal. 3:7–12), gave out of arrogance (Matt. 6:1–4), lied to God about their giving (Acts 5:1–11), put their hope in money

(1 Tim. 6:17–19), or were blinded by their wealth (Rev. 3:17), money has influenced, impacted, and distracted God's people throughout all ages. What we find in each of those passages, and others, is that a desire to "keep" and not "give" is a serious matter to God. No matter the situation, storing up possessions for yourself and not giving away generously is not just a mistake; it is rebellion against what God has called His people to do. As we contemplate the idea of generosity throughout the rest of this book, let me encourage you to heed God's word to Cain: "Sin is crouching at the door. Its desire is for you, but you must rule over it" (Gen. 4:7). If we are to err, let's err on the side of generosity.

From the Old Testament to the New Testament, we find passage after passage informing God's chosen people how they should approach money. We know from Ecclesiastes that those who desire wealth will never have enough, "The one who loves silver is never satisfied with silver, and whoever loves wealth is never satisfied with income" (Eccles. 5:10). Ecclesiastes presents to us the *If You Give a Moose a Muffin* principle.[2] Have you ever read that book? It is one of my children's favorite stories to read at night. It begins with the simple gesture of offering a moose a muffin. The moose then asks for jam to go with it. After the jam, he then wants another muffin, and then another, and another. After eating all the muffins, the moose wants more, so he requests to go to the store to buy all the ingredients. Before leaving he realizes it's cold and needs a sweater, so he asks to borrow one, but that sweater is missing a button and needs to be fixed first. Well, you get the picture now. The moose is never satisfied with what he receives. Once he has been given what he has asked for, he is already thinking about the next thing he "needs." The moose's appetite for the next best thing is never satisfied with what he has; he always wants more. Well, according to Solomon, an appetite for money is never satisfied by money, but only fuels the fire for more, more, and more.

Not only is an appetite for money never satisfied, but we also know that the desire for more money drives mankind to do unthinkable things. It's no secret that over the last few decades money has been the cause of many wars, tragedies, and calamities of all kinds. The apostle Paul poignantly tells Timothy, "For the love of money is a root of all kinds of evil, and by craving it, some have wandered away from the faith and pierced themselves with many griefs" (1 Tim. 6:10). While this verse could be the topic of a book itself, let's briefly look at it together. There are two primary things we must hear from this verse. First, Paul is showing Timothy (and us) that if you were able to look at the fruit produced by evil, and trace down its vine, you would find no other than the craving for money at its root. It's there in the root where the desire for money is nurturing and sustaining the evil it births. No matter what evil is produced, money is often at its core. The root of craving money sprouts the fruit of many evils. Not only is money often at the root of evil, but craving money hinders faith and brings on grief in one's life. I love how Paul echoes the hunger theme from Ecclesiastes here and illustrates the desire for money as a "craving."

When I think of craving, I think of when my wife was pregnant with both of our boys. She did not have a craving for a specific food often, but when she did, that was the only thing on her mind. The craving would become so strong, we would often have to stop what we were doing, get in the car, and go pick up whatever it was she wanted—sorry, *needed*! Whether it was an ice cream cone, sundae, or root beer float, my wife's craving for something sweet trumped all of our other plans for the evening. You see, when a craving strikes, it's the only thing on your mind and it's the only thing you desire.

Unless we are incredibly self-disciplined, we tend to pursue our cravings and put aside all other things until that desire has been satisfied. Just as a fruit can be traced to its root, cravings produce actions in everyone's life, and often that action is seeking to fulfill that craving no matter the cost.

Here's the second thing Paul is saying to Timothy: some have wandered from the faith because their craving for money is the only thing on their mind and it's the only thing they desire. Their desire for money and all of its trappings have consumed them to the point of abandoning their faith. In their pursuit of satisfying the craving for money, they no longer desire faith and godly contentment (1 Tim. 6:6), and in doing so, they have "pierced themselves with many grief" (v. 10). Not only does he use a graphic image to illustrate the way in which they are grieved (being pierced), but that their grief is not singular but qualified by the adjective "many." What type of grief will one experience? By not giving a specific answer, Paul speaks volumes. One can only imagine that the "many griefs" produced by pursuing money will be painful and experienced in numerous ways. Whether it comes in the form of irreparable relationships, loss of wealth and employment, a destroyed reputation, or other consequence, pursuing money for self-gain is a painful way to live. To pursue the craving of money means not only that money becomes your sole focus but it also brings hardship and heartache into your life. Because the craving for money is never satisfied, to pursue it means to dismiss a satisfied life.

How do we fix this craving issue? By craving something greater—contentment. While money itself isn't an unrighteous thing to work for, just like most other things in life, it's our hearts that twist its goodness and hinder us from using it for God's glory. If our main focus is on money and possessing more of it, then pursuing it is an exercise in futility. But if our main focus is on Christ and the gospel, then we are satisfied, and our money and possessions can be used for God's glory.

## WHERE IS YOUR TREASURE?

As I already mentioned, my wife and I have two very young boys. When our oldest son was younger, he had become obsessed with what he called his "tweasure." I am not sure where he picked up that new vocabulary word, but he had an intense and particularly vested interest in his earthly treasures. Whether it was his stuffed Mickey Mouse or Lightning

McQueen car collection, my son was always thinking about and talking about his treasure. He knew where they were at all times and wanted to take them with him everywhere. For my son, his treasures meant everything to him, and he held them very dear to his heart. That may sound silly to us as adults, to treasure children's toys, but we, too, often have treasures that are always on our mind, we know where they are, and we hold them close to our hearts. Our treasures may not be stuffed animals or small die-cast cars, but our treasures are often found where our minds and wallets drift to the most.

While money isn't the number one topic Christ talks about, it received a fair treatment throughout all of Scripture. In the greatest sermon ever given, the Sermon on the Mount, Christ tells His hearers the dangers of an obsession with money and the condition of their hearts. For Christ, how Christians view their possessions is not an unimportant topic by any means. Let's look at Matthew 6:19–24 together.

> "Don't store up for yourselves treasures on earth, where moth and rust destroy and where thieves break in and steal. But store up for yourselves treasures in heaven, where neither moth nor rust destroys, and where

thieves don't break in and steal. For where your treasure is, there your heart will be also. The eye is the lamp of the body. If your eye is healthy, your whole body will be full of light. But if your eye is bad, your whole body will be full of darkness. So if the light within you is darkness, how deep is that darkness! No one can serve two masters, since either he will hate one and love the other, or he will be devoted to one and despise the other. You cannot serve both God and money."

In six short verses, Christ unearths the root of obsession with money—the heart. This passage tells us three equally important issues we should know when it comes to money and where we store our possessions.

## MONEY AS AN ISSUE OF HEART

For Christ, how we handle our possessions and steward our finances is an **issue of the heart**. The first three verses in the above passage encourage the reader to look heavenward when it comes to their possessions. There are only two things you can do with treasure: either store up on earth or store up in heaven. You can't do both. Your treasures, the things you value most, either monopolize your mind on earth or you store up treasure in heaven. Let's not mince Christ's words here, because these verses are not a simple suggestion but an emphatic command. Christ doesn't say, "I think you should consider where you store up your treasures"; He emphatically says, **"Don't!"** when it comes to storing up earthly treasures, and **"Do!"** store up treasures in heaven.

What happens to treasures stored up on earth? Another way to ask that question is: What will eventually happen to your wealth, estate, or prized possessions? Christ presents to us the ever-present reality that all of our treasures on earth will fade. In fact, all things on earth will eventually fade, except for the Word of God (Isa. 40:8). Storing up treasures on this earth is useless because all of the things we possess on earth will either be eaten up, destroyed, or stolen.

Yet storing up treasure in heaven has the opposite result—security and eternity. Heavenly treasures will never experience the clutches of death and destruction. Possessions placed in the heavenly storehouse will never be eaten, destroyed, or stolen. That is where all things are safe, secure, and eternal. In supporting His command to think heavenward when it comes to possessions, Christ tells us that what we do with our treasure is ultimately an issue of the heart. Where your treasure is located, there your heart is also. Christ's words should cut through to us with utmost clarity and force us to ask ourselves this simple question: Is my heart focused on treasures on earth or treasures in heaven?

Paul helpfully orients the Colossian church to know what it means to have your hearts aimed heavenward.

> So if you have been raised with Christ, seek the things above, where Christ is seated at the right hand of God. Set your minds on things above, not only earthly things. For you died, and your life is hidden with Christ in God. When Christ, who is your life, appears, then you also will appear with him in glory. (Col. 3:1–4)

Christian, you have been raised with Christ, and now therefore should be focused on the concerns above, the things of heaven—not the things of earth. To store up treasures in heaven means that your heart and mind are with Christ, who is in heaven seated at the right hand of God the Father (Ps. 110; Heb. 1:1–4). Putting our hearts in heaven means we live with a "now and not yet" focus on the kingdom of God and live in light of Christ's imminent return. As one who has been redeemed by the blood of Christ, you recognize that Jesus is sovereign over all things. And His sovereignty is not stifled by our previous desire for money and possessions.

Where our hearts reside is directly a matter of faith. If we are to listen and apply Christ's words to our lives, then we must acknowledge that our concern is not earthly gain but a heavenly inheritance. Where you store your treasures is an issue of the heart because it states that your heart is either more motivated by the accumulation of possessions, or it is in heaven with Christ. I once had a mentor tell me, "The thing you love the most is what determines how you spend your time, thoughts, and money." His wise words remind me of how Christ calls us to reorient our own hearts. If our treasure is in heaven, and our hearts are there with him, then all of our energy, time, talents, thoughts, and resources on earth are spent for His cause.

## MONEY IS AN ISSUE OF HEALTH

If the original hearers, or us for that matter, didn't feel the weight of Christ's commands in Matthew 6:19–20, then hear what Christ says in the following section. Verses 22–23 move the conversation from an **issue of the heart** to an **issue of health**. Christ says, "The eye is the lamp of the body. If your eye is healthy, your whole body will be full of light. But if your eye is bad, your whole body will be full of darkness. So if the light within you is darkness, how deep is that darkness!" Like the great teacher He is, Jesus gave an illustration that His hearers surely understood; He used the human eye and body as a way to talk about spiritual health. Some may read this entire passage today and think, *These few verses don't seem to fit with what comes before and comes after*, but stick with me here and we will see how Christ's use of the eye lets us "see" the theological truth concerning how we "view" possessions as an issue of health (please forgive the puns).

Your eyes, just like all other body parts, are complex organs. Most of us live every single day without thinking about how they work or the hundreds, if not thousands, of processes they go through just to let us see what is in front of us. Let's do an exercise together quickly. Close your eyes for ten seconds, open them up, and think about all that you see. Go ahead, I will wait. When I opened my eyes I saw my desk, an open Bible, my computer, a hot cup of coffee, and a stack of books. What did you see? For us to see, register, and think about what is in front of us, our eyes work harder and faster than we can even comprehend. In order for you to see once you opened up your eyes, the light in the room hit your cornea to help you focus; light also entered into your eye through your pupil, which is surrounded by your iris, which controls the amount of light let into your eye. Next light hits your lens, which works with your cornea to help focus light correctly into your retina. When light hits your retina, which is at the back of your eye, special cells called photoreceptors convert the light into electrical signals. Those electrical signals then travel from your retina, along the optic nerve, and right into your brain, where your brain turns the electrical signals into the images you see.[3] What only took us a split second to see, our eyes processed in nanoseconds. We can see because our eyes use the light they take in to communicate to our brains what images are around us. When healthy, our eyes give benefit to the rest of our bodies.[4] As biblical scholar Leon Morris points out,

> The eye is the organ that means light to the body; whether we are sighted or blind depends entirely on the eye. The eye is the source of light to the whole body. Apart from the eye the body would receive no light; thus the eye functions much as a lamp does. It is therefore important that the eye be healthy, singly concentrating on its proper function. In that case the proper functioning of one small member means illumination for the whole body.[5]

How your eyes give benefit to your whole body is the illustration Jesus uses to show a spiritual parallel. Jesus says that "the eye is the lamp of the body"; when your eyes are healthy, your body is "full of light." Just as healthy eyes illuminate the rest of the body, in a spiritual sense, our eyes illuminate our lives. If our eyes are letting in light, then our whole body is full of light. Christ is saying, how we focus our eyes—or more accurately, *where* we focus our eyes—determines how we live.

Jesus also presents the exact opposite fact for His listeners, that when the eye is "bad," the whole body is filled with darkness. Without healthy eyes, we can't see properly, and the rest of our body can't rightly function. If you don't believe me, then close your eyes and try to do a normal task you do on a daily basis—even something as simple as brushing your teeth, putting on socks, or pouring a cup of coffee. You may get through it, but it won't be done well and will likely take you longer than normal! What we find in verses 22–23 is a simple equation: a healthy eye equals a healthy body, but a bad eye equals a bad body. It's amazing how such small organs like the eyes determine your health and well-being. Like what James says about the tongue (James 3:1–12), the eyes are a small part of the body but direct where it goes, either to light or darkness. What you think may be small and insignificant, Jesus is saying can actually have the greatest impact on your life.

Looking out from the immediate context of these few verses, we are reminded that Jesus has already spoken on the difference between the earthly and heavenly dynamic. Just as we can either store treasure on earth or in heaven, our eyes can either focus on light or darkness—either on the things of earth or the things of heaven. When our attention and focus drifts to the things of earth (money and possessions), our lives will surely follow. Yet if we lift our gaze and focus our sight on heaven, the rest of our lives will be tuned to desiring God's will and service to King Jesus. A healthy eye produces a properly functioning life. An eye focused heavenward produces a healthy Christian. What is a healthy Christian? One who is investing his or her life in service to King Jesus.

## MONEY IS AN ISSUE OF SERVICE

Christ has shown how money and possessions are both an issue of the heart and an issue of health, and now in the last verse (v. 24) He talks about how they are also an **issue of service**. "No one can serve two masters, since either he will hate one and love the other, or he will be devoted to one and despise the other. You cannot serve both God and money." In each of the previous sections, Jesus gave a parallel between two things. First, it was between earth and heaven, then it was between light and darkness, and now it is between God and money. If anyone was questioning exactly what Jesus was saying in those first five verses about possessions, He is being loud and clear here. Your decision is either to serve God or to serve money; you can't do both. Just as you can either store treasure on earth or in heaven, or be full of light or darkness, you can't have two masters. You can serve one or the other, but both can't have a claim on your life.

While this verse is clear, Christ's analogy still catches us off guard. When we think of money and possessions, we never think of them as our "master." We are the ones working to get the money, we are the ones planning on how we accumulate possessions, we are the ones who choose how we spend our earnings, so we think we are the ones in control. But on the contrary, Jesus speaks directly to the core of the issue and says that when money is your desire, then money is in fact your master. We may think we have everything under control, but it's the unrighteous desire for money that directs our lives. Money demands our time, commands our attention, hinders our health, and rules over us. When we aren't careful, money becomes the master and we become the slave, ultimately serving at its every command. The reality is, we can only have one master, either money or God. Why can't we have both? Because both money and God demand wholehearted service.

So, if both money and God demand our service, what does wholehearted service to God really look like? In Romans,

Paul calls the believers there to stop living in sin (6:1–2). By baptism Christians are signified to be united with Christ's burial and resurrection, to now walk in newness of life (6:4–6); having been crucified with Christ means they are freed from sin (6:7); and finally, because they are united to Christ, they share in Christ's resurrection, being freed from sin to live for God (6:10–11). Because of Jesus's death, burial, and resurrection, those who come to faith in Jesus experience a new life. The believer's life goes from being captive to the darkness and a slave to sin, to now freed from sin and a servant of God. Being in Christ, and united with His death, burial, and resurrection, removes the shackles of sin in one's life. As Paul says elsewhere, "Therefore, if anyone is in Christ, he is a new creation; the old has passed away, and see, the new has come!" (2 Cor. 5:17). Because of the wondrous work of Christ, the newness of life experienced by believers calls them to serve their new master—wholeheartedly.

In Romans 6:1–11, Paul gives Christians the foundation for their service, and verses 12–13 gives them the terms of their service. Let's focus on verse 13. Speaking on the way Christians should serve God, Paul says, "And do not offer any parts of it to sin as weapons for unrighteousness. But as those who are alive from the dead, offer yourselves to God, and all the parts of yourselves to God as weapons for righteousness" (Rom. 6:13). When it comes to service, we must be whole-hearted, or whole-bodied for that matter, for God. We can't be divided and offer "any parts" of ourselves to sin to be used in unrighteous ways. But as those who have been raised from the dead in Christ, we must give "all the parts" of our lives in service to God, for His glory. This is why Christ says that you can't serve both God and money. To divide oneself in an attempt to somehow serve both God and money means you aren't wholeheartedly serving either master. Newness of life in Christ demands believers to turn from the unrighteous pursuit of wealth in order to serve the one who has saved them. Serving both God and money isn't an option—as Christ says, it's impossible. Someone may ask, "Why is serving both God and money impossible?" That's a great question! Charles Spurgeon provides us the answer: "God and the world will never agree, and however much we may attempt it, we shall never be able to serve both. . . . You can live for this world, or you can live for the next; but to live equally for both is impossible."[6] In other words, you can't cling to Christ while refusing to let go of money and possessions. You will eventually let go of one in the pursuit of the other. Just as money is an issue of the heart and an issue of health, money is an issue of service because it tries to master you and pull your attention away from God. You will either be mastered by God and make money a servant for His purposes, or you will be mastered by money and ignore God. Your service to one comes at the expense of the other. You can't serve both God and money.

## HEART, HEALTH, AND SERVICE

Christ is clear: how you view money and possessions is vitally important to your heart, health, and service. You can either store up treasures on earth, be filled with darkness, and serve money, or you can store up treasure in heaven, be filled with light, and serve God. Because of the seriousness of Christ's call to serve God and not money, should we forsake all money and possessions, and live communal lives like religious zealots? No, I don't think that's the answer we find in Scripture. We don't need to look any further than the passage we've already been studying to see how we should understand money and possessions as a means for God's use.

Years ago, when my wife and I were newly married, we drove to Pittsburgh with some friends to go grab dinner at one of our favorite restaurants and then stop by a well-known coffee shop downtown. After having an incredible dinner that was followed up by an edifying conversation and coffee, we decided to head home. It was dark as we drove, and I didn't quite know where I was going. As I drove the four of us home, we got on the highway and barely got out of the city before I was faced with a fork in the road (at least I thought it was a fork). Everyone was talking, so I didn't want to interrupt and ask what to do, so I panicked, made the decision and took the left side of the fork. Within seconds I realized how bad that decision was. I wasn't facing a fork in the road; I had just driven up the wrong way of an off-ramp! As headlights were speeding toward us, I quickly turned the car around and put the pedal to the floor and got us safely off the ramp. Though that was over a decade ago, I will never hear the end of it from my wife and our friends, Scott and Lindsey. Though we laugh about it now, I have always remembered how taking the wrong road and going in the wrong direction put us in a serious situation. Now when driving I always use my GPS and don't trust my instincts. I know every road I am going to take and know where it will eventually end.

This passage presents to us the two roads that can be taken when it comes to money and possessions. And similar to my driving incident in Pittsburgh, these roads either lead to life or death. We can either take one road that points our hearts heavenward where our possessions will never perish, which provides light to our healthy bodies and enables us to joyfully submit in service to God. Or we can take the other road that leads to materialism that doesn't care for the kingdom of God, have sickly bodies full of darkness, and serve money as if it has saved us from our sin. Let me encourage you to have a heart that desires the things of heaven. That kind of heart no longer cares for itself first, but longs for Christ's return and is invested in gospel proclamation here and now. Let me encourage you to have a body that is full of light and not darkness. A healthy body is one that trusts more in the sufficiency of God than the state of the stock market. A healthy body gives generously and knows that God provides for His people at all times and in all things (2 Cor. 9:8) to equip them for every good work. Let me encourage you to serve God alone. When you turn away from serving money, or other idols in your life, you can be wholly devoted to a holy God. Serving one master means that nothing else occupies your time, distracts your attention, requires your energy, or demands your investment. Turning away from money to serve God alone is the most freeing experience one can have in this life. Now your time, attention, energy, and money are used solely for God, His purposes, and proclaiming the gospel to the ends of the earth.

To continue building our biblical and theological framework for giving, we first need to address the elephant in the room: Should Christians practice tithing? In the next chapter we will explore the Old Testament, the Mosaic covenant, and the law to see how tithing is no longer a requirement for believers and how the new covenant calls us to something greater.

## DISCUSS

1. Has your heart been more focused on storing up treasures on earth or storing up treasures in heaven? Is saving money and accruing wealth your end goal?

2. After reading through Matthew 6:19–24, would you consider your view of personal finances and giving to be healthy or unhealthy?

3. In what ways does a biblical understanding of possessions and treasures (money) allow you to serve God well? In other words, who is your master?

4. When it comes to money, what are practical ways for you to develop a heart for heaven, a healthy body full of light, and a desire to serve God alone?

## CHAPTER 3

# Old Habits Die Hard: The Law and Tithing in the Old Testament

*"Don't think that I came to abolish the Law or the Prophets. I did not come to abolish but to fulfill."*
—Matthew 5:17

WE ALL HAVE HABITS. It doesn't matter if it's something simple like going to bed and waking up at the same time every day, ordering pizza for dinner every Friday night, or playing the daily crossword puzzle; we all have developed our own personal habits. Whether your habits are daily, weekly, or even yearly, we often do them routinely without even thinking about them. Think about it: when was the last time you were aware you were going through the habit of getting ready in the morning, checking your email at work, or even reading your Bible daily? Sure, you are aware of those daily routines, but if you tried to change the rhythm in which you do them or break them completely, you would quickly realize how you try to do them without even thinking. Recently I decided to take a brief break from social media so that I could focus on more important things: family, ministry, and work. I deleted my social media accounts and removed the apps from my phone. While my break was only about eight weeks long, I still found myself regularly grabbing my phone to scroll through X (formerly Twitter). Without even thinking, I was inclined to scroll any of my social media accounts even though I was actively trying to take a break from them. After about a week, I realized how much of my daily scrolling was no longer a leisurely practice but a daily habit. Habits, good or bad, are simply routines that our brains have cemented into regular practice.

I didn't even notice how bad my social media habit had gotten until my wife so lovingly pointed it out to me. And that's the thing; habits are typically unnoticed until someone points them out or you try to break them. Without thinking, I would grab my phone, scroll social media, and check my email even though I had just done that less than ten minutes prior. The habit of scrolling on my phone became an involuntary practice. But isn't that the point of a habit? It's a routine you can do without thinking about it. Establishing habits like this aren't typically hard, but it's the breaking of them that is not easy. You may have heard the phrase, "The chains of habits are too weak to be felt until they are too strong to be broken."[1] We don't notice how strong a habit has become in our lives until we attempt to change it. Have you ever tried to break one of your habits? Difficult, wasn't it? Thankfully my 8-week hiatus from social media helped reshape my thinking and break the habit of endless scrolling. But imagine a habit you've had your entire life. How hard would that be to break? I guess that's why they say, "Old habits die hard."

We all need people in our lives who are willing to point out our bad habits that need to be broken. So let me point out a bad habit worth examining. Christians have had a bad habit of using the Old Testament law as the basis for their understanding of giving. Wait! I know how bad that may sound, so before you close this book, call me a heretic, and give me a bad Amazon review, hear me out. The Old Testament is ripe with passages about giving, providing offerings, and instituting the tithe. We can see throughout Israel's history how deeply engrained giving was in their lives. It's no wonder we quickly turn to the Old Testament to established principles for giving in the Christian life. It's so common to do this that we often hear how the Israelites tithed regularly; therefore Christians must follow suit. By looking at the Old Testament and the law, we see how tithing and giving were not only commended by God but commanded by God. While giving was not unique to the Mosaic Law, it was ratified as a requirement under its establishment. Thus, Israel gave out of compulsion to the law, not from a posture of generosity. In studying the Old Testament, many Christians adopt the practice of giving under the Mosaic law, viewing giving as a legal requirement for their faith. Instead of looking at tithing in Israel as a helpful principle, we've made it a habit to see it as a requirement for us today as well. Because we've looked to the Old Testament as our basis for giving, we've perpetuated the habit that giving is a legal requirement for believers still today, instead of viewing giving as a privilege to participate in the glorious work of the gospel.

Through this chapter, I want to show you why we need to break this habit of tithing and see our call to give not as an obligation for our lives but a privilege to participate in. To better understand the change from Old Testament tithe to gospel generosity, we first need to look at the role of the law in the Old Testament, how tithing was practiced in the life of Israel, and how Jesus fulfills the law in order to establish the new covenant. Together, we can let an old habit die and see the beauty of how the gospel calls us to generosity.

## THE ROLE OF THE LAW IN THE LIFE OF ISRAEL

At the beginning of every year when many people begin to read through their Bibles chronologically, they often get stuck in books like Exodus, Leviticus, and Deuteronomy. It makes sense because these are tough books with a lot of rules, regulations, and bloody sacrifices. But I think the most difficult thing about these books is that we encounter God's law for Israel. It's not that reading passages about the law is difficult; it's that as Christians we often struggle with trying to make sense of God's law in our own lives. As we read Exodus, Leviticus, and Deuteronomy, we see that some of the laws are easily understood, like the Ten Commandments (Exod. 20:1–17). But others are just confusing and make us scratch our heads, such as "Do not boil a young goat in its mother's milk" (Deut. 14:21), or "Do not crossbreed two different kinds of your livestock, sow your fields with two kinds of seed, or put on a garment made of two kinds of material" (Lev. 19:19). While some of the laws show us more of a moral purpose, like the Ten Commandments, and others lead to civil or ceremonial function within the community (goat's milk and clothing options), all of the law was of utmost importance in the life of Israel. So, when we read through the early parts of the Old Testament, we ask ourselves, "Does all of the law apply for Christians today?" And then we follow up with, "If not, what laws apply and why not others?" Of the more than 600 laws Israel followed daily, we find the legal requirement to tithe as a major aspect of participating within God's covenant framework. Particularly for our discussion on giving, we want to know whether tithing still applies to believers today. I think to answer that question well, we first must ask ourselves what purpose did the law have in the life of Israel.

The law in the Old Testament can refer to multiple things. In some instances, we see how "law" can be used to reference the entire Old Testament, the Pentateuch (first five books of the Bible), or the commands and instruction that God gave to Moses. Most often, when we hear the term "law" it's in reference to the third option, God's commandments given to Moses for His people. Though God established covenants with Adam, Noah, and Abraham, it wasn't until His covenant with Moses that His law for Israel was put in writing. In each of God's previous covenants, He stipulates how His people are to live and to be in relationship with Him, and the Mosaic covenant was no different. Because of man's sinfulness and because of God's holiness, man could not live in right relationship with God anymore. So, through the law God stipulated how His people were to live, relate to Him, and come into His presence. The law helped Israel understand how they were to love and serve God. This is why it is said that the law was summarized in this passage, "Listen, Israel: The LORD our God, the LORD is one. Love the LORD your God with all your heart, with all your soul, and with all your strength" (Deut. 6:4–5).

God commanded Moses to teach the Israelites to follow and observe the law because it instructed them how to love God. The law and all of God's statutes were then summarized in the command to love God with their whole being. The New Testament affirms this when Jesus and Paul teach that the law given under the Mosaic covenant called for people to love God and love their neighbor (Matt. 7:12; 22:37–40; Rom. 13:8–10).[2] It was their love for God that fueled their love for neighbor (Lev. 19:18). It was the law given to Moses for Israel that clarified how Israel was to love God and live in relationship with Him. Every law they observed could lead them to love God with their heart, soul, and strength. The call to love God, through obedience to His law, required the whole life of Israel. Israel was instructed how to love and serve God through their obedience to the law. The law was Israel's way of life. And much like the Mandalorian moral code, if anyone in Israel questioned their need for the law, the Levitical priests could say, "This is the way." The law enabled Israel to love God, live rightly, love others, and be a witness to the world for God's holiness. The law was not an insignificant thing for God's chosen people. Obedience to the law was quite literally a matter of blessing or curse, life or death, God's presence or His absence, safety within God's promised land or destruction and exile (Deut. 4:25–28; 31:16–17). And of the laws God gave Israel to obey within His covenant with Moses, we find the requirement to tithe. Even tithing was instituted as a law that enabled Israel to live rightly and love the Lord their God.

## ISRAEL AND TITHING

Often when we discuss giving in the church today and someone uses the phrase "tithe," we commonly associate it with the idea of 10 percent. That isn't a poor understanding, because tithe quite literally means a tenth.[3] Naturally, we readily take the tithing principle from the Old Testament and apply it to our lives today. Because we see that Israel gave a tithe, 10 percent, to God, then we must give a tithe, 10 percent, to God through our local church, right? That question isn't as easily answered as one may assume. If we want to break the habit of building our foundation of giving on the Old Testament law, then we must ask ourselves a few questions first. Why did Israel tithe? What did they tithe? How much did they tithe? Lastly, how often did they tithe?

We can answer that first question quickly in two ways. First, as we've already seen, the law was given to rightly orient Israel's life to love God with their heart, soul, and strength, as well love their neighbor. In doing so, the law instructed how God's people were to live and relate to Him. Obedience to the law was the way of life within God's covenant with Israel, and the requirement to tithe was not excluded from this framework. We see in multiple passages in the Old Testament where God commanded His people to tithe of their produce, land, grains, livestock, etc. (i.e., Lev. 27:30–33). Second, Israel tithed because what they had already belonged to the Lord (Lev. 27:30). They were tithing (produce, grains, livestock) to God what was already His in the first place. Israel is to tithe because 10 percent of what Israel had already belonged to the Lord. In fact, that ten percent is considered holy, consecrated, and set apart for the Lord. Since tithing was required under the Mosaic law, it was not an option for God's people. Giving was not based on generosity and out of the abundance of one's heart because Israel gave out of obedience to the law—it was a legal requirement.

As we've already discussed, Israel tithed because it was a legal requirement for them. They gave out of obedience and tithed to God what was already His. As we read through the Old Testament though, we commonly run across three primary purposes for Israel's tithing. Those three tithes, though instituted under the same law, were distinct in their designation and purposes. The first of the three tithes was called the Levitical tithe to support the Levites and priests (Num. 18:20–24). We find this detailed passage about the Levitical tithe and its purpose. In Numbers 18, we find that Israel's tithe was given in support of the Levites and priests. The Levitical tithe is given because God had promised the tenth of Israel's produce, grain, fruit, and animals as an inheritance for the Levites. Unlike the other tribes in Israel, the Levites stood out uniquely. Their call was to be in service to the sanctuary (or "tabernacle" as some Bible translations say), and from within the Levites came the priests. While Israel gained an inheritance of the land and prospered through it, the Levites did not receive an inheritance or portion. In fact, God calls Himself the Levites' "portion and inheritance." Without land or the ability to grow crops or raise cattle, the Levites relied on God to provide for them. Under the Mosaic covenant, this provision was established as law for Israel. Because of their work in the sanctuary, God promised Israel's tithe as their inheritance. Israel was required to give in order to support and sustain the Levites, priests, and sanctuary.

The Levitical tithe, including the priestly tithe, was not the only way Israel gave under the Mosaic law. In the Old Testament we find the concept of a festival tithe as well. Though it is first mentioned in Deuteronomy 12:17–19, it is in Deuteronomy 14:22–27 where the greatest amount of detail can be found. Just as the Lord instructs how to give through Levitical tithe, He also instructs Israel how to give the Festival tithe. Just as Israel was to give a tithe for the Levites, they were also required to tithe for festivals. Now, these festivals weren't your average party. It's not like Israel decided to all "chip in" to help cover the cost of food for their family gathering. No, these festivals were held to commemorate and celebrate God's provision for Israel, while looking back to God rescuing His people out of Egypt. The three main festivals—Passover (Deut. 16:1–8), the Festival of Weeks (Deut. 16:9–12), and the Festival of Shelters (Deut. 16:13–17)—all reminded Israel of God's miraculous redemption from Egypt. The Passover celebrates God's providing salvation to Israel by the blood of a spotless lamb. The Festival of Weeks celebrates God providing the inheritance (the land) to grow produce and raise livestock. The Festival of Shelters celebrates God's provision and protection through Israel's wandering in the wilderness. Each of these three main festivals celebrates God's provision for Israel's exodus out of Egypt and settling into the Promised Land. To celebrate God's redemptive work and provision for Israel, these festivals required Israel to give another tenth of their grain, new wine, fresh oil, and firstborn of their herd and flock. They are to take their tithe to the tabernacle, where God's presence is, and worship Him through a feast. Israel was to feast on their offering as a way to celebrate God's goodness and rejoice with their families. The law required the festival tithe so that Israel would worship God in His presence, remember what God did for them, and celebrate His greatness.

Lastly, the third major tithe for Israel was the charity tithe. In Deuteronomy 14:28–29 and again in 26:10–16, the concept of the charity tithe is given to Israel. The Levitical tithe and the festival tithe were commanded yearly, but here at the end of Deuteronomy 14 the language shifts: It is on every third year that Israel is required to give the charity tithe to go toward providing food and nourishment for the less fortunate. While the charity tithe is still a benefit for the Levites, it also goes to the resident alien, fatherless, and widow, none of which would have been able to provide for themselves. That would be like you and I decidedly giving 10 percent of our groceries each year to the poor and needy within the towns where we live. Essentially, for Israel, the charity tithe went directly to where they lived to support those who did not have an inheritance from God or a means to provide for themselves.

That means that for the average Israelite, the law required the Levitical tithe, the festival tithe, and the charity tithe as regular rhythms and routines throughout the year. The question then must be asked, how much was Israel giving in their tithes? If we are to understand the three tithes as separate and compounding, not in lieu of one, then Israel gave 10 percent yearly to support the Levites, 10 percent yearly for the festivals, and 10 percent every third year for the poor in their communities. That means that every year Israel gave twenty percent of their produce and livestock, while every third year they gave a total of 30 percent of their produce and livestock. If you calculate a rough average, that means every single year Israel was tithing just shy of 25 percent. Let that sink in for a moment!

Through obedience to the law, Israel tithed in order to support each of the covenantal requirements—the priests to mediate for Israel, remembrance festivals of what God had done, and provisions for those without an inheritance. For Israel to live rightly and love God and love their neighbor, they didn't just tithe a paltry 10 percent annually but were obligated to give *beyond* a tenth.

## JESUS AND THE FULFILLMENT OF THE LAW

Our first question we want to address together is this: "Are Christians still under the law?" The answer is an emphatic "No!" Numerous passages in the New Testament witness to that very fact (Rom. 6:14–15; 7:5–6; Gal. 3:15–4:7; 2 Cor. 3:4–18; Heb. 8:13). I intentionally started this chapter by quoting Jesus at the beginning of the Sermon on the Mount. Christ said, "Don't think that I came to abolish the Law or the prophets. I did not come to abolish but to fulfill" (Matt. 5:17). Up to this point, this whole chapter has been explicitly dealing with why the law was established and how the Israelites tithed in obedience to the law. Other than the laws on tithing, Israel had a lot of laws to follow that we find quite odd. When we read through our Old Testament, we encounter many rules and regulations that Israel had to follow that we no longer follow today. For example, if you ate bacon for breakfast this morning then you shouldn't feel as if you had broken God's law (Lev. 11:7; Acts 10:12–16). As we read these laws, we are all particularly pointed back to the Mosaic covenant and the laws established with Israel, to separate them from the rest of the world and to teach them to love God with their entire being. As we've already said, Israel's life was all about the law and strict obedience to it. Their prosperity or demise rested upon their obedience to God's law. But when Jesus opens up His sermon in the Gospels, He clearly states His purpose was not to "abolish" but to "fulfill" the law. But what exactly does that mean? In order to explain what fulfillment of the law means, let's first define what it doesn't mean.

As a father of toddlers, I have had fun watching them grow and develop personalities. But one of my favorite aspects of fatherhood is watching my children react when something isn't working for them. In these moments, you get a glimpse into how they are developing critical thinking and wrestling with frustrating situations. My temptation is to always jump in and help them, but I have to remind myself to sit back and let them try to figure it out first. Our oldest son (four years old) is a very calm and thoughtful child, but when something isn't working the way he wants it to, whether it's a toy or a puzzle, he reacts by saying the same thing every time: "I'm going to throw this in the trash!" He often spends little time trying to figure out the problem; he just knows something is no longer working, so his answer is to throw it in the trash and find something new instead of trying to make it work. (I won't deny he gets this trait from his father!) Because he believes something isn't working, he would rather throw it out instead of trying to make it work.

This might be the way we view how Jesus came into this world to fulfill the law. We think that Jesus needed to fulfill the law because it was ineffective and needed to be thrown out in order to get a new law. But that isn't the case! The law wasn't the problem; it was mankind. The law was good in that it revealed God's holiness and it worked by pointing out man's sin. But it was also not good in that it revealed God's holiness and it worked by pointing out man's sin (Rom. 7:7–25). No, it's not a contradiction to say that the law was both good and bad, because it was not good and bad in the same way. As Paul says in Romans, "The commandment that was meant for life resulted in death for me. For sin, seizing an opportunity through the commandment, deceived me, and through it killed me. So then, the law is holy, and the commandment is holy and just and good" (Rom. 7:10–12). The law was good and holy because it revealed sin, but it was bad because the sin it revealed led to man's death. You see, it wasn't the effectiveness of the law that was in question, but the obedience of man. As Paul says in 1 Timothy 1:8, "But we know that the law is good, provided one uses it legitimately." He continues in those next few verses to say that the "law is not meant for a righteous person, but for the lawless and rebellious" (v. 9), and then provides a long list of sinful acts done by sinful people—all of which needed the law to show them their sin. The law reveals the holiness of God as well as the sinfulness of man. The law calls for perfect obedience, and man is incapable of perfect obedience. So instead of throwing the law away (abolishing it), Jesus fulfilled it. By fulfilling the law, Jesus did not simply toss the law to the side to establish a new way of living. Jesus fulfilled the law in doing what man could not do—obey it perfectly. Let's look at the full context of our opening verses found in Matthew 5:17–18:

> "Don't think that I came to abolish the Law
> or the Prophets. I did not come to abolish but
> to fulfill. For truly I tell you, until heaven
> and earth pass away, not the smallest letter or
> one stroke of a letter will pass away from the
> law until all things are accomplished."

In these two short verses we learn a lot about the Christian's relationship with the law. Jesus does not mince words when He tells His listeners that His purpose is to fulfill the law. As famous biblical scholar Leon Morris says, "*I came* is a significant expression" in these verses.[4] It points the reader to Christ's mission, the fact that God took on flesh, dwelled with His people, died for their sins, defeated death through His resurrection, and ascended into heaven to sit at the Father's right hand. Jesus *came* with a mission. That mission was not to abolish the law, but to fulfill it as the perfect and righteous law-abiding Son of God. In doing so, the fulfillment of the law points us to the person and work of Jesus Christ. This is exactly what Paul wants Christians to understand as he presents the gospel in 2 Corinthians 5:21. It was Jesus who was without sin yet took our sin to the cross and was nailed with our transgressions so that we would receive His righteousness. The perfect and sinless Christ fulfilled the law by being perfectly obedient—even to the cross.

Christ's mission was clear: to fulfill the law. Why did Jesus need to fulfill the law? Simply because mankind couldn't. As the author of Hebrews points out to us, the first covenant had been faultless, and it was God's people who were at fault (Heb. 8:7–8). By quoting Jeremiah 31:31–34, Hebrews shows how God "will make a new covenant" (Heb. 8:8) that is "not like the [old] covenant" (v. 9) He made with Moses after rescuing Israel out of Egypt. In this new covenant, God says, "I will put my laws into their minds and write them on their hearts. I will be their God, and they will be my people" (v. 10), and He will "forgive their wrongdoing" and "will never again remember their sins" (v. 12). In the old covenant God's laws were written on stone, demanding Israel's obedience. Under the new covenant, God writes His law on the hearts of His people, where perfect obedience is found in Christ and His righteousness is extended to believers through faith in Him. Through fulfilling the law, Christ rendered the law in the Old Testament as void. The author of Hebrews summarizes this thought when he says, "By saying a new covenant, he has declared the first is obsolete. And what is obsolete and growing old is about to pass away" (v. 13). In fulfilling the old covenant, Jesus establishes the new covenant. This new covenant, built upon the faithfulness of God and the righteousness and obedience of Jesus, is given to God's people through faith. Faith in what? Faith that is placed in the person and work of Jesus Christ.

## THE WAYS JESUS FULFILLS THE LAW

The question I hear most often from people when teaching and preaching on Christ fulfilling the law is, "If Jesus fulfills the Old Testament law, then why do we still follow some Old Testament laws and not others?" For example, established under the law and old covenant we hear both commands, "do not steal" (Exod. 20:15) and "do not . . . put on a garment made of two kinds of material" (Lev. 19:19). As you read those two laws, you knew the first still stands and yet you are likely wearing clothes made of multiple different types of materials. Regardless, it is a wonderful question to ask, and it is helpful for us to consider as we seek to be obedient to God's Word and faithfully live in service to Christ. I usually answer that question with another question. I don't think the right way to frame the question is to ask, "Why follow some laws but not others?" but it is more appropriately asked, "Does Christ fulfill each of the laws in the same way?" Asking the question in that way allows us to see how some of the laws from the Old Testament are still binding to Christians today, while others are obsolete.

As new covenant believers, we know that all of the Old Testament points us to Jesus. Beginning with Moses and all the prophets, Jesus showed how the entire Old Testament was about Him (Luke 24:13–35). All of the Old Testament is read in light of the person and work of Jesus, including the law. And because we read our Old Testament through the lens of the cross, we can see how Jesus uniquely fulfills the law, in distinct ways. Though Jesus fulfills *all* of the law, not *every* law is fulfilled in the same way and respect. We see that Christ fulfills the law in four primary ways: He maintains it (Deut. 6:4–5; Matt. 22:37–40); He transforms it (Exod. 20:8–10; Matt. 11:28–12:28; Hebrews 3–4); He extends it (Deut. 22:8; Matt. 7:12); and He annuls it (Lev. 20:25–26; Acts 10:12–15).[5] Using those four categories, we can better understand how some laws are maintained in the Christian life today, transformed for Christians to follow, extended for further impact, and annulled to no longer be followed.[6]

Christ does not abolish the law, but He fulfills it. Whether Christ maintains the law, transforms the law, extends the law, or annuls the law, all of these are seen as fulfillment of the law. But I do think it is worth noting something extra before we move on. There may be a theological temptation for us to hear the term *fulfillment* and live as if the law doesn't matter to Christians at all. We don't want to fall into the trap of being a lawless people and living our lives however we please. No matter whether a law is maintained, transformed, extended, or annulled, all of the law is still pertinent for the Christian life. It's not pertinent in the same way it was for Israel, but as Christians we still see all of the Old Testament (the law included) as inspired by God and "profitable for teaching, for rebuking, for correcting, for training in righteousness, so that the man of God may be complete, equipped for every good work" (2 Tim. 3:16–17). Though covenantal stipulations don't drive us to obedience to the law, we can still see all of the law as a way to reveal to us the character of God, point us to our Lord and Savior Jesus, and teach us how to live wisely.[7]

## ARE CHRISTIANS REQUIRED TO TITHE?

This is the question you have been waiting for! You may have even skipped everything in this chapter to get here. If you did, that's okay! But I would strongly encourage you to at least skim through the previous sections because they are what really set up how we understand whether or not Christians are to tithe. So, without delay, let me answer the question for you, "Are Christians required to tithe?" My answer is, "No!" As Jesus fulfilled the law through His perfect obedience, He annulled the requirement to tithe as a measure of man's obedience. To support my answer, let me give you three reasons why Christians are no longer required to tithe.

First, and probably the most important of these answers, is the fact that Christians are no longer under the Mosaic covenant. We've discussed this briefly already, but it needs repeating. God saved His people by bringing them out of exile in Egypt. After leading them out of Egypt, God made a covenant with Moses, stipulating the covenant with required obedience. God said, "Now if you will carefully listen to me and keep my covenant, you will be my own possession out of all the peoples, although the whole earth is mine" (Exod. 19:5). The Mosaic covenant required Israel's obedience. Under that covenant the requirement of tithing was given. Israel tithed as a form of obedience to the law and covenant. Tithing was tied directly to the covenant, both in ministry and promises. Tithing celebrated God's provision in saving Israel out of Egypt, giving them the sanctuary and sacrificial system and land to live in. To be God's people in the Old Testament meant to tithe, as well as follow the other 600+ laws!

The Mosaic law would still be our authority if Christ had not come, fulfilled the old covenant, and established a new one. For Jesus, Paul, and the rest of the apostles, Christians were no longer under the law, because they were under the grace of Christ. Christians have been set free from the bondage of sin and requirements of the law, in order to serve Christ in the freedom He gives (Rom. 6:20–22). For Christians to hold to the requirement of tithing would be to turn back to the Mosaic covenant as the means by which their lives and obedience are measured. They are intentionally enslaving themselves to something from which Christ has indeed set them free.

The second reason Christians are no longer required to tithe is because of how tithes in the Old Testament were used. As God established His covenant with Israel and gave His laws, He instructed them on how to tithe to support the covenant. As stated earlier, the tithes were primarily used for the Levites and priests, festivals, and charity, and all pointed back to God's provision for Israel. These tithes were directly tied to the covenant's work to maintain Israel's holiness (Levites and priests) and to celebrate God's provision in their lives after the Exodus (festivals and charity).

The Levites were called out to be mediators between God and Israel (Exod. 28–29; Lev. 8–9; Deut. 10:8). They served in the sanctuary without ceasing, providing the sacrifices and atonement Israel needed due to their sin and rebellion against God. The Levites and priests were an ordained and consecrated people serving the Lord's commands under the Mosaic covenant. Their role was specifically given for the sacrificial system in the Old Testament. Israel was required to tithe in order to support the Levites' work and ministry of the sanctuary, because the Levites had no inheritance in the land. Because the Levites worked on behalf of Israel, Israel provided for the Levites. As Christ fulfilled the law, He also fulfilled the Levitical and sacrificial system. In establishing a new covenant with God's people, Jesus annuls the previous priesthood to set up a new order of priests. Jesus now serves as our great high priest (Heb. 4:14), and now believers are a royal priesthood. Hear God's word from 1 Peter 2:9: "But you are a chosen race, a royal priesthood, a holy nation, a people for his possession, so that you may proclaim the praises of the one who called you out of darkness into his marvelous light." Did you see how the language of 1 Peter sounded a lot like the language of Exodus 19:5–6? Both passages talk about God's people being His possession, being a kingdom of priests, and a holy nation. The only difference is that one verse is given under the old covenant and the other under the new. Jesus establishes a new covenant that does not require a select priesthood because through faith we all join in the priesthood of believers. Through the new covenant we are a chosen race, holy nation, and God's possession, to proclaim to the world the one who has saved us. The priesthood of the old covenant mediated sins; the priesthood of the new covenant proclaims the saving work of Jesus Christ. Instead of receiving an inheritance of land that yields produce, all believers alike have received their inheritance in Jesus Christ (Eph. 1:11). Therefore, there is no need to give a tithe for the Levites, because the work of the Levites is null and void. Jesus serves as our great high priest (Heb. 8:1–2), who after completing the work of atonement, is now seated at the right hand of the Father in heaven (Heb. 1:3).

Besides the annulling the Levitical tithe, Jesus annuls the festival and charity tithes as well. Just as the Levitical tithe was established under the Mosaic covenant, so were the festival and charity tithes. Where they differ is in their purpose. The Levitical tithe was for the work of the Levites, while the festival tithe and charity tithe were for the purpose of celebrating God's provision in the land He had given Israel. All three of the major tithes are a direct result of God's redeeming Israel from Egypt, establishing a covenant with them to be their God, and providing the land and produce they grow. The festival and charity tithes were a way that God required Israel, by the law, to celebrate His provision and worship Him. These tithes were specific to Israel not just as God's chosen people but as a nation, because they lived in God's Promised Land. Whether the tithe was annually (festival) or every three years (charity), these tithes were a result of God's provision through the land Israel received.

As Christ fulfills the law, the command to tithe and celebrate God's provision through the old covenant and the Promised Land is no longer required for God's people. Because of Jesus, the Promised Land (particularly the sanctuary) is no longer the epicenter for believers. Christians today do not have to go to celebrate and worship God in a specific location (Jerusalem), because God's Holy Spirit indwells all believers (1 John 4:13–15). The land God provided for Israel represents the Mosaic covenant and the law. Now through Christ, a believer's citizenship is not tied to an earthly Jerusalem, but a heavenly Jerusalem (Gal. 4:21–26). We don't look back to the land promised and given under the Mosaic covenant, but we anticipate a coming heavenly kingdom that is unshakable and unending (Heb. 11:10; 12:28; 13:14). God's presence is no longer centralized but is internalized within His people. God does not reside in an earthly temple, but in the temple of His church—every believer. To turn back and tithe for festivals and charity, to celebrate God's provision under the old covenant, would mean to neglect the superiority and greatness of the new covenant established by Jesus. In fulfilling the law, Jesus annuls the festival and charity tithes while also calling Christians to a higher standard—generosity.

The third reason we should no longer practice tithing is because this law has been annulled through Christ's fulfillment. There are many reasons to see the requirement of tithing as annulled by Jesus and the new covenant. First, the New Testament does not command it. Just as we discussed how certain laws are maintained, transformed, extended, or annulled through our readings of the New Testament, we don't find a single instance where tithing is commanded or required of new covenant believers. If tithing were to be required of believers today, then similarly to most of the Ten Commandments, it would have been maintained as the new covenant was inaugurated. Yet, no explicit command, instruction, or law is given to Christians regarding the tithe. While some may look to Jesus's teaching in the Gospels as an affirmation of tithing, upon reading the context you can see how this isn't the case. Tom Schreiner points this out when looking at the passages found in Matthew 23:23 and Luke 11:42.[8] For context, Jesus says to the religious hypocrites of His time, "Woe to you, scribes and Pharisees, hypocrites! You pay a tenth of mint, dill, and cumin, and yet you have neglected the more important matters of the law—justice, mercy, and faithfulness. These things should have been done without neglecting the others" (Matt. 23:23). While Jesus does not denounce the tithe in this passage, He is also not affirming it for believers today. In this passage Jesus showed how hypocritical the Pharisees and scribes were for observing the tithe while neglecting other aspects of the law. Additionally, as we read this passage, we have to position it within redemptive history. We have to look at this passage in relation to the cross of Christ. Jesus is speaking to the scribes and Pharisees prior to His death and resurrection.

At this point in Jesus's ministry, the new covenant had not yet been established, and the old covenant was still intact. The old covenant and its laws were in place until Christ fulfilled them and the new covenant was established (Matt. 5:17–20). Jesus kept the law until His death and resurrection because He was born under the law (Gal. 4:4). As the perfect man and second Adam, Jesus obeyed the law, fulfilled the law, and established a new covenant for His people (1 Cor. 15:45–49).

The second reason we see tithing as an annulled law is because the New Testament does not affirm an ongoing tithe in the new covenant, but it does call Christians to something greater—radical generosity. Instead of calling believers to give a tenth of their money, the New Testament calls Christians to give, and to give generously. These two types of giving are drastically different. Tithing was given as a legal requirement, while generosity is a benefit of the freedom we have in Christ. We see generosity as the model for believers in multiple different ways in the New Testament. Whether it is in the way they live among one another (Acts 2:42–47), share things in common and provide for the needy (Acts 4:32–37; Gal. 2:10), give aid in times of need (Acts 11:27–30), gather a collective offering in our local churches for ministry support

(1 Cor. 16:1–2), or trust in the Lord's sufficiency as they gave (2 Cor. 8:1–9:15), we find generosity in the New Testament as the disposition every Christian is called to as they give. The call to generosity and giving is superior to the command to tithe, because the new covenant established through Christ is superior to the covenant established with Moses. Christians don't tithe because we are called to something greater: generosity that is rooted in the gospel of Jesus Christ.

## IS GIVING AN OBLIGATION, OPTION, OR OPPORTUNITY?

We've talked a lot about the Old Testament, the Mosaic law, and how the law established the tithe. In Christ's fulfillment of the law, we know that it has been annulled and no longer a practice for believers today. That means that tithing is *not* an obligation for believers. But does that mean that giving is simply an option? If you don't mind, let me answer that question by quoting the apostle Paul: "Absolutely not!" (Rom. 3:4). It's unfortunate that giving is viewed as either one of two things: an obligation or an option. This is a false dichotomy. There aren't just two options when discussing giving for believers today. To consider giving as an obligation would be to legalize something that the Bible doesn't command, while considering giving as just an option is to neglect the Christian's call to generosity. Both the obligation view and the option view fail to recognize the superiority of the gospel of Jesus Christ. Gospel generosity is an *opportunity* to display the saving work of Jesus Christ in your life. Gospel generosity reveals the transformation of our hearts and heads, to joyfully give back to the Lord what He has already given us. We don't need to hold on to our earthly possessions and treasures, but we give cheerfully because we know we have "an inheritance that is imperishable, undefiled, and unfading, kept in heaven for you" (1 Pet. 1:4). Our real treasure is in Jesus Christ, who is our "anchor for the soul, firm and secure" (Heb. 6:19). Christian generosity and giving cheerfully lean into the work of the gospel, on the earth until the end of days, because we know that our hope in Jesus is better.

Giving is neither a legal requirement nor just an option for the Christian life. It's an opportunity to proclaim and portray the saving work of the gospel to the world around us. Generosity is a cheerful disposition that rises out of life in Christ and is spurred on by the indwelling Holy Spirit. As theologian John Webster once said, "Generosity is one of the deep and holy things of the gospel."[9] Webster points out exactly what I stated in the first chapter. Christian generosity is rooted in the gospel, which develops a cheerful disposition within the believer, and is done so with the aim of participating in the work of God until Christ returns. Giving is not an obligation. Giving is not an option. Giving is gospel opportunity.

## CONCLUSION ON THE LAW AND TITHING

Was this a long chapter? Yes, yes it was. But I hope you see how necessary it was for us to break the habit of looking to the Old Testament and old covenant as our models for giving in the church today. Through this chapter we looked to the Old Testament to better understand how the old covenant, law, and tithing in Israel are drastically different than that of giving in the New Testament and new covenant. The old covenant was given to Israel through Moses after God saved His people from Egypt. God didn't institute the covenant and laws prior to saving Israel, but He saved them and extended His grace before He established His law and Israel's requirement for obedience. Through the old covenant, God gave the law of tithing as a way to support the Levites and priests, to celebrate Him through festivals, and to give to the needy within Israel's individual communities. The tithe was tied to God's covenant, and for Israel to receive God's blessing they had to obey it. It was in the fullness of time (Gal. 4:4–7) that God sent His Son Jesus to fulfill all that the law required. By His perfect obedience to the law, and His death and resurrection, Jesus fulfilled the law and established a new covenant with God's people. The fulfillment of the first covenant meant that all of its stipulations and requirements find their completion in Christ. Some of the laws Jesus fulfilled by maintaining them, transforming them, extending them, or annulling them. The law of the tithe was annulled by Christ's fulfillment because the necessity of the sacrificial system was made obsolete (Heb. 8:13). God's people no longer needed the Levites, priests, sanctuary, or sacrifices because Jesus serves as our great high priest (Heb. 4:14), is our perfect sacrifice (Heb. 10:12), and has obtained for us an eternal redemption (Heb. 9:12).

Because of Christ's work in fulfilling the law, Christians are no longer required to tithe under the Mosaic covenant. But just because Christians are no longer obligated to give, does not mean that giving is just an option for our lives. Giving is neither an obligation nor an option, but an incredible opportunity to give generously, as those who have been transformed by the gospel. In the next two chapters, we will look together at how the Gospels and the rest of the New Testament call believers to live a life of radical generosity.

## DISCUSS

1. Be honest with yourself; have you had the "bad habit" of thinking tithing still applies to Christians today? If so, what has changed after reading this chapter?

2. Though tithing has been annulled through the work of Christ, do you still think it is a worthwhile principle to follow? If so, is 10 percent the goal, or should we aim for what Israel gave, 20 to 30 percent?

3. Have you ever considered how Christ's fulfillment of the law impacts the way you give generously?

4. What are some ways you can strengthen your understanding and practice of generosity as an opportunity to proclaim and portray the gospel?

## CHAPTER 4

# Giving and the Kingdom of God

*"The time is fulfilled, and the kingdom of God has
come near. Repent and believe the good news!"*
—Mark 1:15

IT WAS ABOUT A decade ago when a few of my friends and
I decided we wanted to go on a hiking trip through the
Allegheny mountains. We planned the trip for a few weeks,
gathered all the necessary gear and supplies, and drove out
to Pennsylvania to start our adventure. We hiked in for a few
hours the first day before setting up for the night. We pitched
our tents, made dinner over a campfire, and stayed up way
too late, worried we were going to be attacked by bears. The
next day we continued our hike, making our way through
tough terrain and sidewinding trails, all while encountering

some unexpected wildlife surprises! As we hiked, we started noticing that the trails were getting less visible and incredibly overgrown, and the trail markers magically disappeared. Did we think anything about it? No, we just kept hiking. We hiked for most of that day before anyone even thought about asking, "Are we going in the right direction?" We finally reached a spot in the Alleghenies where we couldn't go forward any farther and the trail had become treacherous. The trail ended, and we were all standing on the edge of a narrow path on the side of a mountain and the sun was going down. It grew darker and darker by the minute. We were out of our water and there was no fresh water around for miles. We were stuck, stranded, scared, exhausted, and quickly losing sunlight. It wasn't until that very moment someone finally said, "We are lost." The map we had been following had been outdated for decades, and the path was no longer used for hiking. We had walked more than twenty miles without any proper direction! We were aimless and, quite literally, thought we might not make it back out of the forest. Without exaggeration, because we didn't follow the right directions, we almost died in the Allegheny mountains!

Sadly, we often live our lives as Christians just like my friends and I did on our hiking trip. When we become believers, we repent of our sins and trust in Christ's sacrifice to save us, but then we wander around life without any real direction. We think we can go on our Christian hike without guidance and become aimless. We don't think we need directions and start hiking the Christian life without regard for where we are heading. And just like our hike, we usually get pretty far before we realize we are completely lost. As citizens of God's kingdom, we aren't left to walk without direction. The king's people aren't an aimless group questioning whether we are heading in the right direction. We know which direction we are heading because we are following our king (Heb. 12:2). In God's kingdom, Christ the king has given His people direction for all aspects of life—including generosity and giving.

## THE RULE AND REIGN OF KING JESUS

Quick Bible quiz! Do you know what topic Jesus addressed the most in the Gospels? Here's a little hint: it's not money or giving. The theme that Jesus talks about the most in the Gospels is the kingdom of God. Throughout the Synoptic

Gospels (Matthew, Mark, Luke) and the Gospel of John, there are nearly one hundred references to the kingdom of God.[1] Understanding what the kingdom of God is will help us know how living under the rule of Christ calls us to a life of radical generosity.

What exactly is the kingdom of God? We've heard it preached many times in church, talked about it in Bible studies, or read about it during our daily devotions. Yet we still may not be able to define it. Let me give you one of the most succinct definitions of the kingdom of God: "The kingdom is the King's power over the King's people in the King's place."[2] Patrick Schreiner helps to show us the kingdom of God is really about three things: power, people, and place. Specifically, it's about the King's rule and authority (power), the citizens of His kingdom (people), and His kingdom (place). All three—power, people, and place—are necessary to define the kingdom of God, because if you remove one, then the others no longer stand. To have a kingdom you must have a king to exhibit authority over His people in a specific location. A king must rule His subjects within the bounds of His kingdom. The king's authority governs His people within His kingdom. The kingdom is about our King's power (the authority of Jesus), the King's people (Christians), and the King's place (where His power and people reside).

The announcement of the kingdom of God was accompanied by an invitation to become a citizen under the rule and reign of Christ. The announcement of the kingdom of God not only proclaims the good news of the gospel but simultaneously calls for those who hear it to respond in faith—to trust in the saving work of Jesus. To be in the kingdom of God means to live under the rule and reign of the King, under His authority. Just as we once lived in the domain of darkness and followed the ways of our flesh and the spirit of disobedience (Eph. 2:1–3), now as citizens of the kingdom of God we are to live under the king's power and for the king's purposes (Eph. 2:4–10). Through the gospel, we not only find the forgiveness of our sins and redemption, but through the mercy of God we have become "God's people," the citizens of His kingdom (1 Pet. 2:10). In the Gospels, Christ sets forth what living under the King's reign looks like for believers here and now, as well as how we wait for His return. Jesus establishes the kingdom of God and instructs His citizens on how to live under His authority. It doesn't take long to read through any of the Gospels to see how Christ calls us to live as citizens of the kingdom of God. We see how that citizenship impacts every area of life—the way we evangelize the lost, disciple fellow believers, interact with our neighbors, care for our families, live in society, serve God, and minister in our local churches, among many other things. But one thing we can't neglect is how being a part of the kingdom of God affects the way we give. Yes, citizenship in the kingdom of God even impacts our generosity to others.

## GENEROSITY AND THE KINGDOM OF GOD

Christ's rule over His kingdom and instruction for His people impacts every area of life. Nothing is left outside of the sovereignty of our King, including how Christians are to participate in generosity and giving. In the Gospels, Christ teaches us about generosity and how citizens of the kingdom are to give, both to honor Him and to advance His kingdom. But as we read the Gospels and encounter Christ's teachings on giving, we don't find passages that speak to the amount of money that we should give or the frequency in which we make our gifts. No, what we find is the character and disposition behind giving—generosity. While the Old Testament and the law instructed God's people on the amount they must give and the frequency they were to give (20%–30% per annum), Christ's instruction for the citizens of the kingdom of God focuses on something else: the heart of generosity. As we read, we find that the King of the kingdom is more concerned with "why" and "how" His citizens give than "what" they give. The importance of giving isn't the amount someone gives, but the intention behind the gift. The intention behind giving is what points to the character and disposition of the giver. Instead of focusing on the amount someone gives, Christ instructs us about the heart of generosity. According to the Gospels, citizens in the kingdom of God give generously and display their humility, selflessness, and fidelity to the king, instead of proclaiming their wealth, self-righteousness, and arrogance.

The following passages from the Gospels show us how Christ instructs believers to see how giving should be practiced humbly, selflessly, and with fidelity. And as you will see, humility, selflessness, and fidelity also reflect the heart, health, and service of the giver. Instead of being obsessed with possessions (chap. 2), citizens in God's kingdom reflect the effect of the gospel in their lives. In the Gospels, the *character* of the giver is more important than the gift they give. Christ calls for His citizens in the kingdom of God to display gospel generosity, and we do so with a humble heart, a selfless life, and fidelity to service. Through those three characteristics of giving, our generosity not only honors the King but impacts His kingdom. As we seek first the kingdom, let's understand how the gospel transforms the character of the generous giver to be humble, selfless, and committed wholeheartedly to Christ's call.

## GENEROSITY AND HUMILITY

Nothing in this world gives comfort to the burdened, weary to the rest, or peace to the troubled like Christ's call to come to Him. "Come to me, all of you who are weary and burdened, and I will give you rest" (Matt. 11:28). Christ's invitation for us to "come" and trust in His saving work not only provides us with the rest we desire but also calls us to follow after His example. "Take up my yoke and learn from me, because I am lowly and humble in heart, and you will find rest for your souls" (v. 29). Jesus invites those who hear His word to receive His rest and become His disciples. By taking up His yoke, disciples learn from Christ's teachings and follow

His leading. But the call to follow and learn from Christ is not just based upon Jesus's ability to provide you with rest; it's also because of His character. He says that followers should "take up" His teachings "because I am lowly and humble in heart" (v. 29). Why follow Christ's teachings? Because of who He is—lowly and humble. I love how the Scriptures provide us with the little phrase "in heart." Because it lets us know that lowliness and humility are not just temporary actions for Christ but are at the center of His character.[3]

Where is the humility of Jesus found? In His heart. It's from the heart of Christ that we see His lowliness and humility as the basis for following His teaching. Humility is not a temporary action for Christ; it is exactly who Christ is. His very character is marked by His humility (Phil. 2:7). Why should we follow after Christ? Because He is the one who provides true rest *and* the heart of Christ is lowly, gentle, and humble. Christ calls us to find rest in Him and to follow His teaching, which includes His heart for humility. We aren't guaranteed that following Jesus will be easy, but we are certain that followers of Jesus are to be humble in all things. To receive His rest and to abide by His teaching means to commit to following the way of Christ. In the kingdom of

God, citizens are humble because they serve a lowly and humble King. The character of the generous giver has been transformed by the gospel and, in following Christ's teaching, seeks humility. Let's read about the humility of a generous giver from Matthew 6:

> "Be careful not to practice your righteousness in front of others to be seen by them. Otherwise, you have no reward with your Father in heaven. So whenever you give to the poor, don't sound a trumpet before you, as the hypocrites do in the synagogues and on the streets, to be applauded by people. Truly I tell you, they have their reward. But when you give to the poor, don't let your left hand know what your right hand is doing, so that your giving may be in secret. And your Father who sees in secret will reward you."
> (vv. 1–4)

The first characteristic of a generous giver is of humility. Of all the passages in the New Testament that talk about giving, Matthew 6:1–4 is the most direct. It doesn't instruct

Christians on the amount they should give or suggest how often they should give, but it does get to the heart of the giver. It shows us that what matters to God is not the gift given, but the heart of the giver. Just as the heart of Christ is characterized by humility, so is that of Christians. These few verses are split between two sections—first, how one should not give, and second how one should give. Each displays the heart of the giver as well as the response of God.

Verses 1 and 2 are a warning to us, describing how arrogance in giving is not a kingdom characteristic for Christians. Look at that passage again and hear Christ's warning. Giving should not be practiced as a way to display your "righteousness" for others to see. Those who practice giving without humility only care about the applause of man and not pleasing God. They give so that others may see them give. Without humility at the heart of the giver, their motive for giving will never be focused on the King or His kingdom. Humility is always focused on others, while arrogance seeks praise for oneself. Arrogant giving is compared to playing the trumpet before giving, as if you are calling attention to yourself so that others may see you (Matt. 6:2). I played the trumpet when I was younger, and let me tell you, it's not a quiet instrument.

When I was in junior high, I decided I wanted to practice outside one day. I took my trumpet, all my music, and headed out into my parents' backyard. I held up my trumpet and played into an open field. I must have practiced for an hour or so before my mom opened up the back door to the house and called my name. She told me that one of her friends just called on the phone to tell her that my playing was improving and wanted to encourage me. It was a sweet gesture, and it was kindly received until I realized that they didn't live near us. My mom's friend lived about a mile beyond the field in our backyard. I was mortified. Here I am playing my trumpet and even people over a mile away could hear it. I remember thinking, *If she could hear me play from a mile away, then how many more neighbors heard me play "Yankee Doodle" for an hour?* When a trumpet is played, everyone hears it. It draws everyone's attention as it blasts out note after note. You can't help but notice it.

This is what Christ compares the arrogant giver to, someone who blasts a trumpet to gain everyone's attention. Arrogant giving, through the blast of their own trumpet, cries for everyone to "look at me!" Christ warns that giving for the praise of others is seeking the wrong type of reward.

Our reward in giving is not receiving the praise of others but a heavenly recognition from the Father. Giving so that others praise you is not pleasing to God, because Christ says that those who lack humility in their generosity "have no reward with your Father in heaven" (Matt. 6:1). If you give because your heart wants recognition from the world around you, let me warn you: stop! Instead of desiring the praise of others through your giving, seek humility in giving that honors God in heaven.

If arrogant giving is focused on self, then what is humble generosity focused on? Humble generosity does not seek the approval of others, nor does it desire the recognition of all. It does not blast a trumpet to call everyone to attention but gives without anyone knowing. Instead of seeking to be known and applauded, humility in giving only seeks one thing—to be known by God. In contrast to arrogant giving, Christ says that humble giving should seek the approval of one: God the Father in heaven (Matt. 6:4). The act of giving with humility does not care what others may see or think. In fact, Christ says that giving should be practiced so quietly and with such secrecy that even your left hand doesn't know what your right hand is doing (Matt. 6:3). Christ uses this hyperbole specifically as a foil to the arrogant giver. Arrogant givers want everyone to know about their gift, but Jesus says that humble givers are so secret that even part of their body doesn't know they are giving. Humility drives the giver to be so private in their generosity, that even their left hand doesn't know their right hand is giving. So as you give, as Christ teaches, keep the focus on the gift and the one in need instead of yourself and being known by others. Why are these distinctions in giving important? Surely even an arrogant gift is useful for the kingdom. The gift isn't the focus for Christ; it's the character of the giver that must be transformed by the gospel. It is only by humility that God recognizes our generosity. When we give without seeking to be praised, the Father "sees" and we will receive our reward in heaven (Matt. 6:4). Christ shows us that humility and generosity are not used as a way to point to yourself, but to display the saving work of the gospel in your life. With a heart of humility, generous giving only wants to point to one person—Jesus Christ.

## GENEROSITY AND SELFLESSNESS

The second characteristic of giving in the kingdom of God is selflessness. Don't confuse this with selfishness, because these two terms are polar opposites. Though they each contain the word *self*, their definitions couldn't be more different. Each of their definitions has a focus on someone but is aimed in a different direction. Selfishness is focused on oneself instead of others, and selflessness is focused on others instead of oneself. My wife and I have been working through these two ideas with our young sons lately. Almost daily we are having to handle a situation where one of our sons snatches a toy from the other one's hands. And every time we ask, "Why did you do that?" we hear the same response, "Because I wanted it!" There's no regard for his brother, but only a focus on his own joy of playing with a toy. Each time we get to explain what it means for us to be selfless and care for each other as a family. You see, selfishness only wants what's best for the individual instead of seeking to care for others. Selfishness is always focused on "me, me, me," whereas someone who is selfless finds their greatest concern for others. A selfish person sees their life as the greatest priority, but a selfless person puts the lives of others above their own. In the Gospels, we see that Jesus is the perfect example of a selfless person: someone who puts the lives of others above His own, even to the point of death. Jesus even calls us to follow Him in a life of selflessness as we care for others. He tells us in the Gospel of John, "This is my command: Love one another as I have loved you. No one has greater love than this: to lay down his life for his friends" (John 15:12–13). If we are going to love each other just as Christ has loved us, then we must put the concern of others above our own. As the perfect selfless Savior, Jesus laid down His own life for the sake of others. In following Christ's command, we are to be selfless and care for others more than ourselves.

Just as humility is a characteristic of a generous giver in the kingdom of God, so is selflessness. Not only does generosity in the gospel call us to give with humility, but it calls for our giving to be focused on others. We don't give in order to be known, but to put the needs of others first and point people to Jesus Christ. Selfless generosity cares about the needs of others, even above your own. Let's read Luke 21:1–4 together:

He looked up and saw the rich dropping their offerings into the temple treasury. He also saw a poor widow dropping in two tiny coins. "Truly I tell you," he said. "This poor widow has put in more than all of them. For all these people have put in gifts out of their surplus, but she out of her poverty has put in all she had to live on."

This story is a perfect example of what it looks like to be a generous and selfless giver. We find a widow who gives a gift that is above and beyond in comparison to the wealthy people around her. No, her gift may not equal the amount given by the wealthy, but according to Jesus, her wealth isn't defined by what she gave but by her character and disposition in giving. The widow displays a truly selfless act in giving because she gave everything she had. Again, we see how Jesus highlights the character of the giver over the gift in this story. The emphasis isn't on the amount of money that was given, but on the heart and intentions of the giver. Jesus sees two different types of people dropping off their gifts to the temple treasury—the selfish and the selfless.

In the first century, the temple in Jerusalem was not just the central location of worship for Israel but was a repository for wealth.[4] Israelites would come to the temple and drop off their offerings, as well as pay dues and taxes, make other monetary and non-monetary donations, or store their wealth. The money that Israelites gave often was turned around and redistributed to those in need. People often brought their wealth to the temple because they believed that a sacred place was a safe place to use as a repository.[5] It would have been a common practice to see people regularly going to the temple treasury to give a gift. On this particular day, Jesus saw the wealthy give their offerings and a widow give two coins. In observing this, Christ says that all the gifts given by the rich, the widow's gift surpasses in wealth (Luke 21:1–2). It's striking to me that the comparison we find is not between a singular rich person and a singular poor widow. Did you catch that when you read the passage? Jesus says, He "saw the rich" and "a poor widow" giving their offerings. The "rich" is not a singular person but is a plural term and is likely referencing *all* the wealthy people who gave their gifts at the temple treasury. He is calling out *all* the rich in their giving. In comparison to the rich, Jesus uses the singular example of one poor widow to show how the character of giving surpasses the gift itself.

In giving her two coins, Jesus says that the widow had given more than all of the rich combined. Now, I know I am not a mathematician, but how is it possible that all of the wealthy people's gifts to the temple treasury are outweighed by the meager two coins of the poor widow? It's simple, Jesus tells us, "For all these people have put in gifts out of their surplus, but she out of her poverty has put in all she had to live on" (Luke 21:4). The widow, by no means, had any wealth that could be flaunted. To emphasize this, Jesus calls her a "poor widow," really impressing into His hearers the state of the widow's finances. At this time, widows would have been considered among the most vulnerable people in the community. They would not have had a source of income, and without an extended family to care for them, they would have been left to fend for themselves. This is why we hear the command to care for widows and orphans so frequently in the Scriptures (Acts 6:1–7; James 1:27; 1 Tim. 5:3–16). But Jesus says the poor widow gave more because she gave everything she had. Unlike the wealthy people giving gifts, the widow didn't just give a gift; she exhausted her account to give. The widow had only two coins to live on, and instead of keeping them for herself, she gave them to the temple to be used in the service of God. The widow's act of generosity shows her selflessness in giving. As Jesus says, she did not give out of her "surplus" but out of her "poverty."

It is really easy to give out of a surplus. That's because the surplus is never something we truly need. A surplus is nothing more than the money left over after you have paid your bills each month. If you are like me and you pay attention to your budget, then you know exactly how much money you will have in surplus at the end of each month. That money isn't needed to survive; it's simply the leftovers. This is what Jesus says the rich had given out of, their surplus. For the rich, the leftovers are what they deemed acceptable to give because they first took care of themselves. It's like our saying to God, "You can have the leftovers of what I have." For the rich in this story, the surplus wasn't money they needed, nor was it difficult for them to give. Contrary to this type of giving, selflessness in generosity pursues the care of others over one's own needs. The amount of the gift doesn't matter to God, but giving that cares for others is of supreme importance. Or as Charles Haddon Spurgeon once said, "Our gifts are not to be measured by the amount we contribute, but by the surplus kept in our own hand. The two mites of the widow were, in Christ's eyes, worth more than all the other money cast into the treasury."[6] As we practice generosity, our concern should not be whether or not our needs have been met first before we give. But in laying aside our own needs, we see the priority of others and give selflessly. What honors God in giving? A selfless heart that gives out of what one has and not out of one's abundance.

## GENEROSITY AND FIDELITY

The last characteristic of a generous giver is fidelity. And as the old Baptist preacher would say, "That's a $5 word," meaning it is complex and uncommon. Most often, fidelity is simply used as a synonym for faithfulness. It is not incorrect to see their likeness in definitions, because after all the word *fidelity* comes from the Latin word *fides*, which means "faith." So, it's easy to see how one could use them interchangeably, but where I draw their distinctions is in their application.

So what exactly is fidelity? The Christian characteristic of faithfulness in Scripture is tied directly to the faith of a believer (Gal. 5:22; Heb. 10:23; Rev. 2:10), the object of their faith, Jesus Christ (John 3:16; Rom. 5:1–21), and God's faithfulness to keep His Word (1 Cor. 1:9; 2 Thess. 3:3; 2 Tim. 2:13; 1 John 1:9). Those who are faithful are the ones who have put their faith and trust in the saving work of Jesus Christ. Fidelity, though somewhat synonymous with faithfulness, communicates a loyal commitment to following a mission. It's not that these two terms are entirely different, but they show us shades of the nuance of what it looks like to be a Christian. We are faithful to Christ our Savior, and we have fidelity to His call over our lives. I think we see this example clearly in the Gospel of John as Christ calls for His disciples to love Him and follow His commands. "Jesus answered, 'If anyone loves me, he will keep my word. My Father will love him, and we will come to him and make our home with him. The one who doesn't love me will not keep my words. The word that you hear is not mine but is from the Father who sent me" (John 14:23–24). There is a lot we could unpack in these two short verses, but what is glaringly obvious is how there is a clear connection between those who have faith (anyone who loves Jesus) are the ones following Christ's word (fidelity to His call). Those who have faith also have fidelity to the mission Christ has called us all to. You can't be faithful without a sense of fidelity, and vice versa. If you have truly placed your faith in Christ, then you strive to have fidelity to Christ's commands. We follow His Word because we have trusted in His power to save and redeem us. Fidelity is fueled by faith. Fidelity is the outworking of our faith. In many ways, this is no different than how James tells us that "faith without works is dead" (James 2:26). Faith that does not follow Christ's commands with fidelity is not faith at all.

This is exactly why I chose to use the term *fidelity* in this section, because it brings about a seriousness that we often don't hear when we talk about faithfulness. Fidelity loudly communicates active obedience to a specific mission. So when I say that fidelity is a characteristic of Christian generosity, I don't want people to hear me question their faith in Christ if they aren't currently practicing giving on a regular basis. Practicing generosity is not a saving act; only placing your faith in the work of Christ will save you. Since generosity is rooted in the gospel and is a fruit of new life in Jesus, then giving is an outworking of your faith in Christ. Generosity is a tangible way we can proclaim to those around us that we have been transformed by the gospel of Jesus Christ. It shows a change of heart and reorientation of resources to be used in honor of God and for His glory. So, when we discuss fidelity, I am simply explaining that one of the three characteristics of a generous giver is someone who actively pursues the mission Christ has given to believers. Fidelity through generosity is not something I have made up because I think it sounds good, but I believe the Gospels present to us a clear call to fidelity as we pursue a life of radical generosity. As citizens in the kingdom of God, we submit to the King's power and authority with fidelity. Let's take a look at the story of the rich young ruler as an example of how Christ shows us fidelity to generosity as a characteristic of Christian giving:

> As he was setting out on a journey, a man ran up, knelt down before him, and asked him, "Good teacher, what must I do to inherit eternal life?" "Why do you call me good?" Jesus asked him. "No one is good except God alone. You know the commandments: 'Do not murder; do not commit adultery; do not steal; do not bear false witness; do not defraud; honor your father and mother.'" He

said to him, "Teacher, I have kept all these from my youth." Looking at him, Jesus loved him and said to him, "You lack one thing: Go, sell all you have and give to the poor, and you will have treasure in heaven. Then come, follow me." But he was dismayed by this demand, and he went away grieving, because he had many possessions. (Mark 10:17–22)

Now I know what some of you may be thinking: this passage isn't directly about giving like the other two passages we've studied. Up to this point, we've seen how Christ calls us to humility in our generosity as we give without seeking worldly recognition, and we've seen how the poor widow exhibits selflessness as she gives everything she has for the sake of others. The passage about the rich young ruler isn't directly about giving but is about following Christ. Though the passage of the rich young ruler doesn't give us a detailed example of giving, it still shows us indirectly how gospel generosity exudes fidelity to following Christ in all things, including giving. Mark 10:17–22 shows us that to inherit eternal life and to be citizens of the kingdom of God, we must be willing to abandon all of the trappings of this world—including our money. Fidelity requires commitment, and as we see from the rich young ruler, we must be willing to prize Christ more than our possessions.

Every single time I read this passage, I stop and think about my fidelity to Christ. I ask myself, *Have I abandoned all to follow my Savior?* Or I may ask myself, *What areas of my life am I valuing more than Jesus?* And I hope that you too read through this passage and thought about your fidelity to following Jesus. These aren't odd questions to ask yourself when reading this passage, because this is exactly what Jesus intended for us to do when we hear about the rich young ruler.[7] He wants us to reflect and think, *Have I abandoned all else in pursuit of following Jesus?* In asking these questions of ourselves, we are looking behind our actions to know our intent and to evaluate our character. Fidelity to Christ's call to follow Him requires us to put Him first. This passage on the rich young ruler speaks to the character behind giving. And we learn from this passage that following Jesus is greater than our possessions.

Even the rich young ruler asked an important question when he approached Christ. And his question, just like ours, gets to the character behind his actions. The rich young ruler ran to Jesus Christ, the Savior of the world, kneeled before Him, and asked Him what he must do to inherit eternal life. I don't want to spend too much time speculating about the young man's motive or desire, but I think the passage is telling us something specific about him. He didn't just casually walk up to Jesus and talk to Him like a peer, but "ran" and "knelt" before Jesus, showing Him respect and honor.[8] The rich young ruler addresses Jesus as the "good teacher" and asks about eternal life. And the passage later says that Jesus looked at the young man and "loved him" (Mark 10:21). Just from these few observations, it's fairly safe to say that the rich young ruler was genuine in his question and truly wanted to know what one must do to enter the kingdom of God. He seemed to recognize the authority of Jesus and desired to follow His command. Responding to the rich man's question about eternity, Jesus quoted back to him a handful of the Ten Commandments. We know that obedience to the law saves no one, and only by faith in Christ does one enter the kingdom (John 3:16; Rom. 6:23; Eph. 2:8–10). So why would Jesus quote just a few of the Ten Commandments as if the law could save us? I think the answer lies not in the use of the Ten Commandments themselves, but in the specific Ten Commandments Jesus recited. You see, Jesus didn't start with number one and work His way through all ten but reminds the rich young ruler about numbers five through ten. Each of these commandments speaks directly to our relationship with others. These commandments all show us how to care for and interact with others. Christ reminds the rich young ruler "do not murder; do not commit adultery; do not steal; do not bear false witness; do not defraud [the action of coveting someone else's possessions]; honor your mother and father" (Mark 10:19). By quoting these commandments, Jesus is not suggesting that obedience to them earns eternal life, but He is addressing the character of the rich young ruler. He is asking, "Do you care for others?"

As we've already studied together, Jesus tells us elsewhere that the Old Testament law is summarized as loving God and loving neighbor (Matt. 22:34–40). Paul also emphasizes this when he says, "For the whole law is fulfilled in one statement: 'Love your neighbor as yourself'" (Gal. 5:14). Jesus quotes these commandments to the rich young ruler to question whether or not he indeed cares for his fellow man. Quickly, and probably quite boastfully, the young man responds to

Jesus with, "Teacher, I have kept all these from my youth" (Mark 10:20). The young man at this point is probably wiping the nervous sweat off of his brow and saying, "Whew! I've done it!" He asked Jesus what he needed to do to enter the kingdom of God, and because of his obedience to the law, he believes he will inherit eternal life. But this is where the rich man's joy turns to sorrow. Jesus doesn't let the man revel in his self-righteousness but points out the one thing he is lacking—fidelity. To obey these commands means to actively pursue caring for others. Jesus gives four commands to the rich young ruler: "go" "sell" your possessions, "give" to the poor, and "follow" Me (v. 21). By following these four commands, Jesus says, "you will have treasure in heaven" (v. 21). This time, the rich young ruler had a different response to Jesus's teaching. Instead of responding in affirmation and joy, he was "dismayed" and left "grieving" because his wealth was great.

Why did the rich young ruler grieve over Christ's command to give? Because his wealth meant more to him than following Jesus. The young man may have desired eternal life, but not enough to give away his wealth. The rich young ruler was committed to obeying God, but up to a limit. The moment his wealth came into question, he was no longer willing to remain committed to Christ. He no longer desired treasure in heaven but desired his treasure on earth more. In the end, the rich young ruler did not have fidelity to Christ's call. He was not willing to commit his whole life to the cause of Christ, to care for others, and to give generously. His possessions meant more to him than following Jesus. We see here, and through the rest of the Gospels, that fidelity requires giving up everything in pursuit of Jesus (Luke 9:23–27). Fidelity matters to generosity because it means that following Christ is more important than the wealth you have. Giving should not be an issue for those who follow Christ, because earthly treasures pale in comparison to the wealth we have in heaven. If following Christ means giving away every dime you have, then you do so generously, knowing that your real wealth is in heaven.

This passage points us to fidelity to Christ's call to follow Him with our whole life. Jesus tells the rich young ruler he is lacking because if he truly understood what it meant to love his neighbor, then generosity would not be an issue. If the young man followed the commandments as he said he did, then he would not grieve over giving away his possessions, but joyfully and generously provide for the poor knowing that his treasure is in heaven (Mark 10:21). Those with fidelity to Christ's call to follow Him don't grieve over giving but see it as an opportunity to be generous and aid those in need. We can give all that we have because all that we need is in following Jesus.

There's an old story about how John Chrysostom, an early church father, faced severe persecution from the Byzantine empress, Eudoxia.[9] The story—though we don't know if it actually happened or not—is still a helpful way for us to see how fidelity to Christ's call means that earthly possessions are no longer our prize, but experiencing eternal life is. The empress threatened to banish Chrysostom, drive him away from his friends, and kill him. With each of her threats, he retorted with exuberant fidelity to God. But the line that sticks out to me the most is when the empress threatened to take away Chrysostom's wealth and treasures. His response displayed his deep conviction to cherish Christ and His kingdom more than his possessions. Chrysostom answered the empress's threat by stating his treasure is in heaven, and that's where his heart is. The empress's threat posed no real issue for Chrysostom because he knew where his true treasure was. His earthly possessions were of no value to him because following

Christ was his greatest possession, and that could not be taken from him.

Both the rich young ruler and Chrysostom faced a crisis over their wealth, but each responded differently. What made these two stories different? One grieved over the potential loss of his wealth, while the other would gladly let his wealth be taken from him. The rich young ruler valued his money more than following Christ, but Chrysostom saw his true wealth in Christ. The rich young ruler would not give away his possessions to follow Christ, but Chrysostom's earthly possessions were of no value to him compared to his faith in Christ. The call to follow Christ requires us to have fidelity—a desire to actively pursue Christ above all things, including our money. For those in the kingdom of God, generosity is marked by a joyous fidelity, ready to give because following Christ is our greatest possession.

## CONCLUSION

As we studied generosity through humility, selflessness, and fidelity, did you notice the one thing that each of those characteristics have in common? Humility, selflessness, and fidelity all point to the heart, health, and service of a Christian. Our problem with giving is rooted in our sinful obsession with possessions and looks at the heart, health, and service of every individual (chap. 2). It would be impossible to give with humility if your heart were not set on heaven. It would be impossible to give selflessly if your spiritual health didn't see others first as a priority. It would be impossible to have fidelity in giving if you did not have only one master, King Jesus. We could keep turning each of these characteristics around and see how humility is an attribute of our health, selflessness is an act of service to Jesus, fidelity is an action rooted in our spiritual health, and so on. The characteristics of a generous giver display the heart, health, and service Christ commands of His followers. As citizens of the kingdom of God, Christ calls us to give generously with humility, selflessness, and fidelity. Our focus in this chapter has primarily been internal. It's been internal because we've looked specifically at the character of what gospel generosity looks like in the believer's life. In the next chapter, we will explore a more external focus on generosity. We will turn from the characteristics of the giver to the actions of giving itself. We will answer the question, "What does it look like to give as we wait for Christ to return?"

## DISCUSS

1. Have you ever considered how your citizenship within the kingdom of God impacts the way you live and give?

2. When you give, what is your motivation? Do you give so that others may see your gift, or do you give so that others may benefit? Humility in generosity is a heart check for Christians.

3. Selflessness is an act of giving that prioritizes others over yourself. When giving, who is on your mind first, yourself or others?

4. Fidelity is an important characteristic of kingdom giving because it is a commitment to Christ's command. Are you willing to follow Christ even through giving your money and possessions?

## CHAPTER 5

# Generosity in Light of Christ's Return

*Our citizenship is in heaven,
and we eagerly wait for a Savior
from there, the Lord Jesus Christ.*
—Philippians 3:20

ONE OF MY FAVORITE parts of my work week is going home. No, I don't hate my job and count down the hours until I can go home and get away from work. I love going home because of how my two sons greet me when I get in the house. Every single day it's the same exact scene. The moment I get out of my car, I can hear them screaming in the house, "Daddy is home!" Before I can even take my shoes off, the door opens, and both boys are standing there with great excitement, ready to leap into my arms. For them, my return home means everything to them. Once they know that I am coming home, they anticipate my return with incredible joy and eagerness to see me. It's the highlight of my day because I know my sons love me and await my return every single day. I know that this is likely to change as my boys get older, but for now, I relish in the moment.

The childlike excitement I see in my boys daily is nothing more than a glimpse into the reality of how Christians wait for Christ to return. Though we may not know the day or hour of Christ's second coming (Matt. 24:36), we still eagerly anticipate when He will return. Our excitement for Christ's return mimics the joy of my children because we not only love Christ but also know that upon His return the effects of sin will cease (Rev. 21:4). As Christians, we long to proclaim joyfully and tearfully "Christ is here," as He returns to gather His people (Matt. 24:31) and establish the new heaven and the new earth (Rev. 21:1). We are excited and eagerly anticipate His return because we know that when Christ comes again then all things will be made new (Rev. 21:5). Our focus is not on "earthly things," but on the future, imminent, and glorious return of Jesus (Phil. 3:19–21). As citizens of the kingdom of God, we wait for our King's return, both diligently and joyously.

How exactly do we wait on Christ's return? As we anticipate the return of Christ, we don't simply wait around sitting on our hands. When we read the New Testament, we find many passages that speak to awaiting Christ's return. And every time we encounter one of those passages, we not only see a glimpse into waiting, but instruction on how to live now. I think we often hear the word *waiting* and immediately correlate it to something like visiting the DMV. When you go to renew your license or get new plates, all you can do is enter the queue and wait for hours. But this isn't the type of waiting we hear Christ call believers to in the New Testament. Awaiting Christ's return is active. We don't sit passively waiting, but we actively anticipate Christ's return. This type of waiting is diligent and prepares (Matt. 24:43–44; Mark 13:33–36), is faithful (Matt. 24:45–51), committed (Matt. 25:1–13), and glorifies God (Matt. 25:14–30). How we wait on Christ is as important as the act of waiting itself.

Focusing on Christ's return isn't just on "then and how" but also on the "here and now." What I mean is, we don't just look to the future discussing what happens at Christ's return, but we think about how we are to live now according to His future return. Our understanding of Christ's return motivates us to live today. As we wait for our "blessed hope" (Titus 2:13), we remain committed to the task before us (1 Thess. 5:6), knowing that our work is not in vain (1 Cor. 15:58). Therefore, the important question we must ask ourselves is, "How do we live in anticipation of Christ's return?" The answer is quite simple: we live as those who have been transformed by the gospel and empowered by the Holy Spirit, to faithfully follow Christ's Word until He returns.

## GENEROSITY AND CHRIST'S RETURN

When Jesus ascended into heaven, He did not leave us alone without direction as we wait. When we open our Bibles to the book of Acts, we find one of the most encouraging passages concerning Christ's ascension and return. Chapter 1 begins with the ascension of Jesus, where He is "taken up" into the heavens (v. 9). The ascension is an encouraging topic itself for the believer, but it's what Jesus says prior to His ascension that we cling to as encouragement for today.[1] While Jesus was still with the apostles (v. 2), He speaks about the kingdom of God (v. 3) and commands them not to leave Jerusalem and wait for the Father's promise—the Holy Spirit (v. 4). Before He ascended into heaven, Jesus gives a final encouragement to His apostles that as the Holy Spirit comes, they will be empowered to fulfill the commission Christ has given them— proclaim the gospel to the ends of the earth (Matt. 28:18–20; Acts 1:7–8). As the apostles are looking upward, "two men in white clothes" (Acts 1:10) admonish them, saying, "Men of Galilee, why do you stand looking up into heaven? This same Jesus, who has been taken from you into heaven, will come in the same way that you have seen him going into heaven" (v. 11). Though Jesus has gone up into heaven, He will one day come back again. As we wait, God sends His Holy Spirit to us—to guide, instruct, and empower. As Christ ascends into heaven, the Holy Spirit descends to the earth to dwell within His people (Rom. 8:11; 1 Cor. 3:16; Eph. 1:13; 2 Tim. 1:14). The reality is, the coming of the Holy Spirit is not an insignif- icant event for believers. Because as the Holy Spirit descended, we see His work in empowering believers (Acts 1:8), but also how He serves as the "Counselor" for Christians (John 16:7) convicts the world of sin, righteousness, and judgment (John 16:8), and also reminds believers of Christ's teachings (John 14:25–26). Without the Holy Spirit dwelling in believers, we would be lost as we anticipate Christ's return. As we wait for Christ's return, we don't do so as those lost without direction, because we have the Holy Spirit, who indwells, empowers, and instructs us on how to live and obey Christ's Word.

As we learned in the last chapter, giving is an important part of the Christian life. In establishing the kingdom, Christ instructs His followers how to live in the kingdom. Generosity is the way of the King's people, in the King's place, under the King's authority. Just as the Gospels and the kingdom of God speak directly to the character of generosity, giving generously reflects how we wait for Christ to return. Just as the gospel transforms our hearts, minds, and pocketbooks for generosity, the Holy Spirit empowers us to live generously in light of Christ's return. Through the indwelling of the Holy Spirit, Christians are empowered not just to give, but to give generously. What does it look like to give generously as we anticipate Christ's return? The following sections teach us what gospel generosity looks like as we wait for our beloved King Jesus to come back.

## GENEROSITY AS AN ACT OF GRACE

In chapter 1, I defined *gospel generosity* as "giving that is rooted in the saving work of Jesus Christ." More so, it is the Christian's joyful awareness of what Christ has done for them and how they are privileged to participate in proclaiming the work of Christ through giving and advancing the gospel. And according to the apostle Paul, true gospel generosity is an act of grace given to the church. It's an act of grace because it is something we receive by God's grace and then extend out to others as we generously give. In many ways, giving is nothing more than a gift given to the church to be exercised until Jesus Christ returns. Yes, you heard me right. Giving is a gift we have received through the gospel, and the power of the Holy Spirit, to give back to serve God until the Lord returns. Giving isn't something we can contemplate doing, but as the Macedonians show us, it is something we earnestly desire to participate in (2 Cor. 8:4). Because giving is an act of grace, we must not ignore it or let that muscle atrophy. If we heed the Holy Spirit's words through Paul to "excel" in giving (2 Cor. 8:7), giving must be active, exercised regularly, and developed throughout our whole lives. Let's look at that key verse from

2 Corinthians to better understand how giving is an act of grace—it's from God, to the church, and for others.

> Now as you excel in everything—in faith, speech, knowledge, and in all diligence, and in your love for us—excel also in this act of grace. (2 Cor. 8:7)

As we see in this verse, giving is an act of grace. I don't know if there is a better way to summarize or define Christian giving than to say it is an act of grace. But what exactly does it mean for something to be an act of grace? Giving isn't the only thing in the New Testament defined by the term *grace*. As we know, our very salvation is an act of divine grace (Eph. 2:8). God, through Jesus Christ, redeems His people, not as a result of man's work but as a free gift. Grace is nothing earned but is a gift given freely by God. Similarly, giving is an act of grace because it has been freely given to us, to be given back to others. Paul, using the language of grace, instructs the Corinthian church on generosity that is rooted in the gospel. Above all else, Paul shows that giving is a grace given by God (2 Cor. 8:1) that is built upon the gospel of Jesus Christ (2 Cor. 8:9). He wants the church to know that giving is enabled because of the gracious gift of God that is found in the cross of Christ. Christians can give, and give generously, as they wait for Jesus to return because God first gave graciously to them.

In chapter 8 verse 7, Paul does something interesting that we shouldn't miss. Why should we live a life of gospel generosity until Jesus Christ returns? Because giving is a gift given to the church and should be exercised in the same way that we grow in our faith, speech, knowledge, diligence, and love. I don't believe that Paul intended to provide us with an exhaustive list of gifts in this section, because he says to "excel in everything" before providing his prime examples of gifts given to the church. We can look back to Paul's first letter to the Corinthians to see how things such as faith, speech, knowledge, diligence, love, and more are gifts bestowed upon the church by God. God gives these gifts freely so that no one is lacking as they wait for Jesus Christ to return (1 Cor. 1:4–9) and are to be used for the common good of mankind (1 Cor. 12:7). We also find in Paul's letter to the Romans how giving generously is one of the many gifts that God gives to His people (Rom. 12:8). Gifts are given by God to equip the church, as they wait for Jesus and are used for the good of others. God gives the gifts, the church uses the gifts, and others benefit from the gifts. What I fear, though, is that many of us have never considered how generosity is a gracious gift from God to the church for others. I believe this is why Paul instills in the Corinthian church, just as you grow and excel in the other gifts God has given, don't neglect to give because it is also an incredible act of God's grace. The church is not encouraged to be stagnant in these gifts but to excel in all of them. As Christians wait for Jesus to return we are to use the gifts that God has graciously given to us, as a means to fulfill the work He has called us to, and to aid those within the church and outside of the church. Giving, in many ways, should not be pushed aside and neglected compared to the other gifts we see Paul encourage the church to excel in. But we should earnestly desire to grow in giving, just as much as we do faith, love, knowledge, diligence, and speech. Giving is not just a gracious gift of God but a gift that equips the church to serve Him in His work until Jesus returns (Col. 3:23–34). Generosity is our response to God's gift in our lives.

## THE CHEERFUL, GENEROUS GIVER

What accompanies the act of grace of giving in the Christian life? It's the disposition of cheerfulness! Why do these two things go hand in hand? It's because when someone understands that generosity is an act of grace that has been given by God, they are cheerful in how they give. God has graciously given us salvation in Jesus Christ and has equipped us for good work; therefore, we are cheerful in using our gifts to give to others. Cheerfulness always accompanies generosity when giving finds its foundation in the gospel of Jesus Christ. Just as the character of the giver is defined by the gospel, so is the behavior that it produces. Gospel generosity produces cheerfulness because Christians can't help but be joyous in giving as they participate in the work God has given them.

Growing up, I really loved watching the Muppets. I loved the TV show, the old reruns, and all the movies they made. To be completely honest, and much to the chagrin of my wife, I still love the Muppets and I think all the original movies are funnier than ever (sorry, Kelsey!). But one of the characters that always stuck out to me was Sam the Eagle. He was incredibly disciplined and always lecturing the rest of the

Muppets and the audience about something. Sam was incredibly serious, stuffy, and he never laughed. Sam's stoic look and countenance communicated his behavior, no matter what he was doing. You knew that when Sam showed up that some self-important speech was coming. Sam had no joy for life. And by all definitions, Sam was not a cheerful Muppet. Do we approach giving the way Paul prescribes or do we give as if we are Sam the Eagle? Do we give cheerfully as those who have experienced the grace of God, or do we give as those without any joy in their lives? Scripture does not describe gospel generosity as a stuffy practice but as a cheerful participation. Cheerfulness accompanies the generous giver because their joy is found in Jesus, the Savior of the world who will come again. Giving isn't a dreadful practice but a joyous participation. Continuing in 2 Corinthians, we see how Paul, through the Holy Spirit, teaches us that cheerfulness naturally follows generosity:

> The point is this: The person who sows sparingly will also reap sparingly, and the person who sows generously will also reap generously. Each person should do as he has

decided in his heart—not reluctantly or out of compulsion, since God loves a cheerful giver. (2 Cor. 9:6–7)

Immediately following his teaching on excelling in giving as an act of grace, Paul instructs the Corinthian church on how they should give, as those waiting for Christ to return. By giving them an analogy for giving, Paul points the Corinthian church to sowing and reaping as a farmer. This basic farming analogy is not hiding a secret meaning—it is out front for all to hear. If you sow sparingly, you reap sparingly. But if you sow generously, you will reap generously. Paul is communicating to the Corinthian church, and us, the disposition of the giver. Those who give sparingly holds their gifts tightfisted and are unwilling to give abundantly. They risk the overall harvest because they sow out their seed with reluctance. They will not experience a generous return when their crops are ready to be harvested. But those who are generous in their sowing will indeed experience an equal return on their gift.[2] They plant their crops, not holding back any seed, so their harvest is plentiful. Sowing is directly tied to reaping. You will not reap more in your harvest than you planted, nor will you sow everything you have and harvest next to nothing.[3] Whatever you sow, whether little or a lot, you will reap from its harvest. I can see how some might read this passage, interpret the analogy, and think that giving leads to prosperity. No, I don't believe that is what Paul is saying at all. He's not trying to get you to give more so that you reap a great blessing from the Lord.[4] The focus isn't on reaping but on sowing. If your motivation for giving is based on what you may get in return, then you aren't giving as God calls us to do. Do we sow generously so that the impact of our giving will be a large harvest? Or, do we sow sparingly without consideration for the harvest at all?

After challenging the Corinthian church to consider how they give (sowing and reaping), Paul immediately addresses the core attitude of giving for individuals—their heart. No matter the amount of the gift or the frequency of giving, Paul says that believers must decide for themselves how much they will give. I love how Paul says "in his heart" as he teaches on individual giving. Not only does this address the intention of a gift, but Paul emphasizes the personal nature of individual giving. Unlike in the Old Testament, where Israel gave according to the law, Paul says that giving under the law of Christ is determined by the individual. No matter how wealthy or poor they were, Israel was required to tithe. But here in 2 Corinthians, Paul says that apart from any external influence or law, Christians are to determine in their own heart how much they are to give. Knowing that whatever you sow you will reap, Christians determine their giving on an individual basis, not by the standard of the law, but between themselves and God. The reason why giving is determined in the heart of the individual is so that giving is not done so "reluctantly" or "out of compulsion" (2 Cor. 9:7). What produces a cheerful giver? The ability to determine one's own giving out of their heart. Both reluctance and compulsion lead to joyless giving. If you are under compulsion to give, then you feel forced and unable to decide on your own. If you are reluctant to give, then you are hesitant to give and do so without generosity. Paul wants Christians to give neither under compulsion nor reluctance, because God loves a cheerful giver. As Spurgeon once said, "Cheerfulness is the sunshine of the heart."[5] Cheerfulness is an overflow of the heart that has been transformed by the gospel of Jesus Christ. Ultimately, our cheerfulness and joy are focused on the hope we have in Christ's return, not on the possessions we have on earth.

Christians cheerfully give until Jesus returns because they are eager to participate in what God is doing here and now.

## JEHOVAH JIREH: THE LORD WILL PROVIDE

Cheerfulness not only happens when Christians eagerly participate in giving to God's work until Jesus returns, but it is rooted in their ability to give by trusting in the Lord's provision. Cheerfulness naturally occurs when someone can give on their own accord without requirement or reluctance, as well as when they see God as their ultimate provider. This type of giver can cheerfully and generously give, knowing that God will provide for their needs. Christian generosity is an act of trust. It displays our trust in the Lord to provide even as we give cheerfully and generously at the Lord's command. We can give because we know that God will not let us go without.

As you've probably guessed at this point in the book, I am a big fan of Charles Spurgeon. We even named our family dog Charlie after the Spurge himself. There are many reasons why I love reading Spurgeon's sermons, but what always stands out to me is his great faith to trust in the Lord. Even in giving, Spurgeon knew he had to ultimately trust in the Lord and rely on His continual provision. One day in the late 1800s, Charles Haddon Spurgeon was riding in a carriage with his American friend William Hatcher. As the carriage approached Spurgeon's orphanage, he pointed out the window and said, "Yonder is my bank, where I get my money for taking care of my family of 500 children." Hatcher looked around but didn't see a bank near them. But Spurgeon said, "There it is," pointing to a plaque. The words on the plaque read, "Jehovah Jireh," meaning "the Lord will provide." Spurgeon continued, "That is my bank. It never breaks, never suspends, never gets empty. My children have never lacked for covering, or for food and I have no fear that they ever will."[6] Spurgeon knew that whatever he did—start a college, open an orphanage, or even pastor his church—he must trust in the Lord to provide his every need. Do you want to guess what happened in Spurgeon's ministry? He was never without the financial means to pursue what God had called him to do. At one point, Spurgeon even said, "The support of the College [Spurgeon's College] is derived from the free-will offerings of the Lord's people. We have no roll of subscribers, although many friends send us aid at regular intervals."[7] Spurgeon's greatest strategy for fundraising in ministry was to fall to his knees and pray for God to provide. Spurgeon never wavered in his faith nor worried how his ministries would survive, because he knew that God was his provider. Spurgeon's faith in ministry and giving trusted in God to sufficiently give him what he needed. Throughout his entire life and ministry, Spurgeon proclaimed, "Jehovah Jireh," trusting that the Lord would provide for him in all things and at all times.

Charles Spurgeon's incredible faith in the Lord to provide is exactly what Christian generosity looks like. If you've ever read anything about Spurgeon, then you know that his aim in life was not to get money but to give money. And the more generous he was, the more generously God provided for his ministries. Spurgeon knew that no matter what he gave away, Jehovah Jireh would provide for his needs. As the Lord calls us to give generously and cheerfully, He does so with the promise that He will never let us be in need. The Lord, as Jehovah Jireh, enables us to excel in all things until Jesus returns because as we give, He gives back to us in all things. Let's see how the apostle Paul teaches the Corinthians to trust in God's kind providence as they live a life of gospel generosity until Jesus returns.

And God is able to make every grace overflow to you, so that in every way, always
having everything you need, you may excel
in every good work. As it is written: "He
distributed freely; he gave to the poor; his
righteousness endures forever." Now the one
who provides seed for the sower and bread for
food will also provide and multiply your seed
and increase the harvest of your righteousness. (2 Cor. 9:8–10)

These few verses are packed with encouragement for
believers to trust in God's provision as they give generously.
Right before these verses Paul teaches the Corinthian church
about cheerfulness in generosity (2 Cor. 9:6–7). Giving displays the cheerful heart of the generous giver, portraying the
saving work of Jesus Christ in their life while serving God and
others. But Paul also wants the Corinthian church to know
that giving and generosity are products of one's ability to trust
in the Lord for all things. Cheerful and generous givers don't
see their money and wealth as their sufficiency but look to God
as the one who provides for their every need. If there is a verse

in this chapter that defies our cultural ethos today, then this is the one! We live as if our entire lives and needs are only met by our ability to provide. Even as Christians, we trust in our own ability to provide; we pick ourselves up by our bootstraps, work hard, and hoard our money. Because we think if we freely and generously give, then we won't have what we need to survive. This is exactly the opposite of what Scripture tells us! We can give generously without worry for our needs because Jehovah Jireh will provide. It's a healthy and helpful reminder, to know that our sufficiency is not in our wealth but in God. Because as Paul shows us, God is the one who is able to provide (2 Cor. 9:8). Who is the one who is able to make all things overflow in you? If you answered with a resounding "me," then think again. Only God can provide to you every grace, so much so that they "overflow" in and through you. We are generous in what we give because we know that God is the one who makes grace overflow in our lives. And how does God do that? This is one of my favorite lines in all of 2 Corinthians, so don't miss it! As you give, God provides by making every grace overflow to you "so that in every way, always having everything you need" (2 Cor. 9:8). Did you catch that? If not, read it again! *As you give, God provides for you in every way.*

A more literal translation of the Greek text would say that God provides for you "in all things, at all times." Let that reality and truth soak deep into your heart. Even when we feel as though our needs aren't met or we see the plight of others and wonder if God is doing what He said He is going to do in their life, we can rest in His provision. It may not be what we expect or even what the world may tell us we need, but God, who is our portion, is enough, and it is out of an overflow of His goodness to us that we are compelled to live as cheerful givers. It's out of this overflow that we are able to take our eyes off of our needs and place them on the needs of others.

God provides and sustains all of His people as they give generously, at all times and in every way. No one is excluded from the Lord's kind provision as they live out their calling to gospel generosity. No matter your circumstances or station in life, God will provide so that you have everything you need. Whether you are walking through the darkest valley of your life, or you are destitute and don't know where your next meal is coming from, or you are selflessly serving in the villages of Africa or the slums of India, God will meet your needs in every way and at all times. Because even in the midst of suffering and turmoil and even death, those who generously give show their trust in God to provide for them. Generosity, as an act of faith and trust in God, shows our greatest need—God Himself. Just like the Levites in the Old Testament, Christians live as those without an earthly inheritance trusting in their true portion—God (Num. 18:20–24). That's because He, above all else, is what we need. And as our perfect portion, while we remain here on earth, God perfectly provides for us by meeting our needs and equipping us for every good work.

What is it that God provides for us? He always provides for us grace in every way so that we may "excel in every good work" (2 Cor. 9:8). God is not providing our needs to make us millionaires or wealthy beyond measure. No, God provides grace in every way, so that we are never lacking to excel in good work. As we generously give, we trust in the Lord to provide, so that we can continue working until Jesus returns. When we are serving the Lord, we never have to question whether or not we have what we need, because God provides grace in all things, at all times, for the sole purpose of equipping us to serve Him. This is not a unique idea in the New Testament, because we see regularly how we are God's workmanship created for good works (Eph. 2:10), how man is complete and equipped for every good work by the Scriptures

(2 Tim. 3:16–17), that we walk worthy of the Lord as we bear fruit in every good work (Col. 1:10), and that God equips us with everything good to do His will (Heb. 13:20–21). As we give, we know that God will give back to us so that we can continue to serve Him. As Hudson Taylor so helpfully reminds us, "God's work done in God's way will never lack God's supply." When we generously give, God generously supplies us with what we need to do His work.

## THE MINISTRY OF GENEROSITY

Take heart, brothers and sisters; giving is an exercise in trusting the Lord to sustain your needs in life, at all times, in all things. Our giving is rooted in the gospel, is practiced with humility, selflessness, and fidelity to God, and also is an act of grace that cheerfully gives by trusting in God's kindness and care for His people. But what exactly is the ministry of generosity? How should our giving be focused? At this point, we've not talked about the practicalities of giving or discussed where we are to give our money.

Let's consider two big-picture questions for gospel generosity. First, as we give, we must ask ourselves, "Am I serving the Lord?" And second, "Am I worshipping the Lord?" These are questions we shouldn't ignore as we excel in the act of giving. Generosity isn't something we should practice without considering how our gifts are being used and whether or not it honors God. As we wait for Jesus to return, I believe these two important questions about generosity help us focus our giving and seek to glorify God.

Humor me again with another story about Charles Spurgeon. He once said, "Let each man find out what God wants him to do, and let him do it, or die in the attempt. In what way can I bring my Lord most glory, and be of most service to his church while I am here? Solve that question, and pass into the practical."[8] For Spurgeon, his concern with following God's will was answered in two questions: What brings God the most glory? How can I be of most service to His church? If you can answer those two questions, then the rest of your life flows from them as a practical response. Spurgeon's approach is no different than how the apostle Paul instructs the Corinthian church to give. The same two questions Spurgeon asked concerning God's will are exactly what we should ask ourselves when considering generosity. How can I best serve God through generosity? How can I most glorify God through generosity? If we can answer those two questions concerning giving, then, as Spurgeon said, we can pass into the practical. Let's read Paul's word from 2 Corinthians 9:11–12:

> You will be enriched in every way for all gen-
> erosity, which produces thanksgiving to God
> through us. For the ministry of this service
> is not only supplying the needs of the saints
> but is also overflowing in many expressions
> of thanks to God.

Until Jesus returns, the ministry of gospel generosity is twofold: it is for service and worship. It is aimed at serving the saints while also glorifying God. Gospel generosity is "enriched" in every way because of the lavish grace of God. God enables believers to give generously, all for the purpose of doing every good work—supplying the needs of the saints and glorifying God in the process. God initiates generosity by first giving us all that we need. In return, we give generously to serve Him and glorify Him in all that we do. How can we best serve God through generosity? The New Testament is not short of ways in which we can serve through generosity. The ministry of generosity is aimed at service in many ways.

We know from the passage above that generosity is used to supply the needs of the saints (2 Cor. 9:11–13), but it is also used to share what we have and show hospitality to others (Rom. 12:13); support our pastors, elders, and ministry leaders (1 Tim. 5:17–18); reflect our faith in Christ by providing for the poor (James 2:15–17); advance the gospel through missions (Phil. 4:15–19); display God's love as we have compassion for fellow believers (1 John 3:17); support brothers and sisters in the faith, even when they are strangers to us (3 John 5–8); and meet the needs of the widows and poor (Rom. 15:25–27; 1 Cor. 16:1–4; Gal. 2:10; 1 Tim. 5:3). The ministry of generosity lives by the scriptural maxim that "it is more blessed to give than to receive" (Acts 20:35). In all things, at all times, generosity seeks to serve others as believers use the resources God has given them to provide for the needs of individuals, the church, and missionaries, all while glorifying God throughout the entire process. Generosity seeks service that is oriented toward others, and is lifted up to God in worship.

One of the most convicting things I've ever read on generosity and service came from the eighteenth-century pastor and evangelist, John Wesley. In discussing wealth and generosity, Wesley did not mince words when considering how one should give their money. Wesley said, "Do you not know that God entrusted you with that money (all above what buys necessaries for your families) to feed the hungry, to clothe the naked, to help the stranger, the widow, the father-less; and, indeed, as far as it will go, to relieve the wants of all mankind? How can you, how dare you, defraud the Lord, by applying it to any other purpose?"[9] This quote has time and time resounded in my head as I think about generosity and money. Every time I look at our budget, how we spend our money, and how we give, Wesley is screaming at me, "Is this serving others or yourself?" Wesley is right to point out our sinful inclination to focus on ourselves and not others when we consider giving. If we truly recognize the gospel as our foundation for giving and know that God will provide us with our needs, why would we want to put our money to any other use? We must remember: the money and resources that we have, are given to us by God, and therefore how we spend, save, and give money are gospel issues. As you consider giving, think about what John Wesley said and ask yourself, "Will giving serve the Lord, and will it glorify the Lord?" If you can't answer that question with an unequivocal "yes!" then don't do it. Because it is God who supplies our every need, we can in turn give generously to supply the needs of others. We serve others through giving because God has equipped us, by His grace, to do the work of generosity. The one who equips us for the ministry of generosity is the one whom we glorify as we give. How does generosity glorify God? It glorifies Him as we serve others because it points to the Lord's remarkable work in the gospel. It's only by the life-changing transformation of the gospel that believers desire to serve others through giving their wealth. As we give, we glorify God and become a testimony to His saving work in our lives. As we give generously, God receives glory generously.

## ALL THINGS IN COMMON: MORE THAN MONEY

At this point in the book, if you still think generosity is merely about money, then I haven't done a good enough job communicating that the call to generosity is about more than money. Generosity is not just about how much money we give; but it's about a life that is wholly impacted by the gospel and entirely dedicated to its service. Every aspect of a believer's life is to be used generously, to bring God glory and to be used for the benefit of others. As we live in anticipation of Christ's return, generosity affects every area of our lives. From the way we live, work, give, and interact with others, Christ's return motivates us in how we serve and honor God in our waiting.

Before we move on, there's one more thing we need to consider as we think about generosity in light of the return of Christ. Generosity is more than just giving someone cash or writing a check to support your church, missionaries, or non-profit organizations. As we contemplate how we live and give as we wait for the Lord, we must also consider how generosity impacts the way we give our lives wholly in service to God and others. In other words, we need to think about how generosity calls us to share what God has given us—our time, abilities, possessions, and lives—with others. Generosity isn't just about giving one's stuff but giving oneself for the glory of God and benefit of others. Sharing our time, possessions, and abilities is a crucial piece of generosity in the life of the Christian—especially as we anticipate Christ's returning and making all things new. Generosity transcends giving money and includes how we share the God-given abilities, talents, time, and possessions we have.

In my personal opinion, I think that sharing is one of the most difficult lessons to learn in life. It's difficult because no one, no matter their age, wants someone else to have their stuff, let alone use it. Our obsession with possessions drives us to the point of selfishness that cannot see past our own wants and needs. Selfishness makes us all become versions of Gollum from *The Lord of the Rings*. Our possessions, time, and talents are "precious," and we couldn't imagine anyone else having what is ours. We hold those things closely while keeping others at an arm's length away. We aren't willing to share because we think that our possessions, money, time, and abilities are first and foremost ours, and neglect to realize that all we have belongs to the Lord (the earth is the Lord's [1 Cor. 10:26]; all our gifts come from God [James 1:17]).

In many ways, sharing is the antithetical action of selfishness. Sharing is a willingness to let others have and use something that isn't theirs. Maybe sharing isn't difficult for you, but my wife and I are living in this scenario daily with our two toddlers. There are two words no one has to teach a child to say when they start to speak. The first word is "no," and the second word is typically "mine." And when it comes to teaching our boys to share, we regularly hear "no" and "mine." Our boys, and the rest of toddlers everywhere, have this sixth sense ability to know when a sibling is touching their stuff, or even just looking at it (parents, you know what I am talking about). My wife and I have to remind our children that we don't fight over our possessions but share them. What one sibling has, the other can use too. We hold things, especially toys, in common in the Harris household.

Even as adults many of us still feel the temptation to say "no" and "mine" when someone wants to use our stuff, borrow our time, or ask us for help. The only difference is we are mature enough to say, "Now really isn't a good time" instead of kicking and screaming "Mine!" Or if you do end up sharing something, you do so with incredible reluctance and worry the whole time whether your possession will come back exactly as it was when it left or thinking about how you could have spent your day doing something else instead of sharing your time and abilities. It doesn't matter whether you let your neighbor borrow a tool, a family member borrow your car, or you help a friend unload a moving van; we tend to view our possessions, time, and abilities as more important than the relationships with the people who are in need. And just as my kids need regular reminding about the importance of sharing, let me gently remind you now that sharing is the generosity of one's own possessions, time, and abilities for the common good of others. By sharing, a generous person meets the needs of others with the resources and possessions they have. Sharing requires selfishness to be put aside so others may benefit from what you have. Do you want to know what healthy generosity and sharing look like? Look at Acts 2 for an example of how sharing seeks the needs of others while holding possessions in common:

> They devoted themselves to the apostles' teachings, to the fellowship, to the breaking of bread, and to prayer. Everyone was filled with awe, and many wonders and signs were being performed through the apostles. Now all the believers were together and held all things in common. They sold their possessions and property and distributed the proceeds to all, as any had need. Every day they devoted themselves to meeting together in the temple, and broke bread from house to house. They ate their food with joyful and sincere hearts, praising God and enjoying the favor of all the people. Every day the Lord

added to their number those who were being
saved. (Acts 2:42–47)

This passage is an early image of how the church functioned together, caring for one another's needs, and eagerly
waiting for Jesus to return. What makes this passage difficult
for us is knowing how we should read and interpret it for us
today. Scholars either say this passage is prescriptive, meaning that it prescribes a certain way for Christians to live; or
descriptive, meaning that this passage only describes what
the early church did in the first century. If we understand it
as prescriptive, then we take this passage as a command and
directly apply it to our lives. That means we all go out and sell
all of our possessions, live in a Christian commune together,
attend church daily, and worship God as we wait for Jesus. If
the passage is merely descriptive, then whenever we read it, we
gain a head knowledge of how the church functioned without
any heart application. I think choosing between those two
options only gives us extremes at both ends of the spectrum.
Perhaps this passage isn't simply a prescriptive or descriptive
passage but can include aspects of both of those categories. As

we read Acts 2:42–47, we can both understand the church's history and gain a principle of application for us today.

It's amazing to read this passage because it really speaks to the way that the gospel transforms the lives of those who hear and respond to the Word of Christ. The believers who are spoken of in this passage were said to be "devoted" to the apostles' teaching (v. 42), which was handed down to them from Christ (Matt. 28:18–20). The community was devoted to the Word of Christ under the authority of the apostles and lived lives that reflected a radical transformation. You see, they weren't just devoted to God's Word, the breaking of bread, the fellowship, and prayer, but they also were so radically changed by the gospel that they sold all they had so they could *share* everything in common (Acts 2:45). The believers were so moved by the gospel that they no longer prized their possessions, time, or abilities, but saw all they had and owned was to be used to build up one another. Do you understand what that means? Just as the early church was devoted to the Word of God, they were also devoted to one another. If that verse didn't hit you like a ton of bricks, then read it again. The believers in Acts did not prioritize themselves in life but used their possessions, wealth, time, and talents for the benefit of others. They shared what they had so that all could be held in common together. The gospel of Jesus Christ reoriented their thinking to go from selfish individuals to those who put one another and the community first. No one's possessions were solely their own but were for the mutual benefit and edification of the community. Individualism and selfishness were laid aside because the gospel transforms believers to emphasize others' needs over their own. What was the result of gospel generosity in the early church? Sharing that met the needs of the community. Just a few chapters later in the book of Acts, we see another example of how generosity and sharing affects the needs of a community.

> Now the entire group of those who believed were of one heart and mind, and no one claimed that any of his processions was his own, but instead they held everything in common. With great power the apostles were giving testimony to the resurrection of the Lord Jesus, and great grace was on all of them. For there was not a needy person among them because all those who owned lands or houses sold them, brought the

proceeds of what was sold, and laid them
at the apostles' feet. This was then distributed to each person as any had need. (Acts
4:32–35)

Yet again, the gospel is the catalyst for generosity and
sharing in the church. Acts 2 shows us how believers were
devoted to the Word of God and were devoted to one another;
Acts 4 gives us the result of what gospel generosity looks like
when believers give and share. The believers in Acts 4 were
united, both in heart and mind, and valued the needs of others as more important than their own individual needs. I love
how both passages, Acts 2 and Acts 4, tell us that the church
held (shared) all things in common. If you are wondering what
that phrase means, then you are making it more complicated
than it needs to be. To hold all things in common as a community means they were just living the old phrase, "What's
mine is yours." What everyone had (their time, talents, and
treasure) was used for the betterment of the community.
Whatever possessions you had, the property you sold, or the
money you saved, was held in common and used to build up
those in need. Whatever abilities you had were shared among

those around you. Your time was not your own but was used as a resource for the community of believers. The believers were united in holding all things in common because they did not selfishly hoard what they had, but freely shared all things. As the believers held all things in common, something beautiful took place in their community: "For there was not a needy person among them" (Acts 4:34). By sharing what God gave to the Christians in Acts, the needs of the community were met entirely! The generosity of believers transformed by the gospel not only supports one another but shared so that no one was found needy. Sharing selflessly is an indicator of gospel generosity.

If these passages share both prescriptive and descriptive elements, then how should we apply what we read to our lives today? I want to answer that question with another question. Has the gospel impacted your generosity not only to give but to see how sharing can meet the needs of those around you? Beyond financial resources, how can you use the gifts God has given you, your time and abilities, to serve those around you? Though we may not be called to sell all our possessions and live together as the believers did in Acts 2 and 4, we can still give and share as those who care about the community's needs over our own. Gospel generosity that leads to selfless sharing desires to see that there is "not a needy person among them" (Acts 4:34). Gospel generosity calls Christians to live as if "What's mine is yours, and yours is mine," faithfully waiting until Jesus Christ returns.

## CONCLUSION

How we wait on Jesus Christ to return is just as important as what we believe about His return. We aren't intended to neglect the work before us but press on in faithfulness as if we are serving the Lord in all things (1 Thess. 5:6; 1 Cor. 15:58). Jesus calls us in the Gospels (Matthew, Mark, Luke, and John) to live generously as we follow Him. Just because Jesus has ascended into heaven doesn't mean the work of generosity has ceased. As Christ ascended to sit at the Father's right hand (Ps. 110:1), He sent the Holy Spirit to be mankind's Counselor (John 14:26). As God now dwells within His people by His Holy Spirit, He also empowers us and equips us to serve Him in all things. Generosity and giving are not excluded from the Spirit's empowerment in the lives of believers, as we patiently and eagerly wait for Jesus to return.

While we wait, generosity must be seen as an act of grace, given by God to be given unto others. It develops a cheerful disposition in the believer as one who does not give under compulsion or reluctance, knowing that all they have is a blessing of the Lord. Generosity exhibits a steadfast faithfulness in the Lord to provide for all things, at all times in the life of a believer. Through generosity, God equips believers to do every good work, ready to serve Him in whatever He calls us to do. And lastly, generosity enables selfless sharing that values the needs of the community above one's selfish desires. As we wait for Jesus to return, we will continue in the work of gospel generosity, exhibiting character that has been shaped by the kingdom of God and actions that faithfully proclaim the cross of Christ to the world around us.

## DISCUSS

1. How does Jesus's return affect the way in which you live? Does it motivate you to serve Him faithfully, or does it cause you to freeze in fear?

2. Have you ever considered how the indwelling Holy Spirit empowers you to live today? Through the Holy Spirit's power, we pursue holiness and live a life honoring of God. But sometimes the Spirit's work in our lives is also of conviction. As you read this chapter, were you convicted at all about generosity? If so, how?

3. How can you cultivate a disposition of cheerfulness in giving?

4. If you were to be honest with yourself, or those around you, would you say your generosity and giving reflect your trust in God to provide for you? Do you give generously but also fear whether or not you have the means to survive?

# Generosity and Portraying the Gospel

*"Because of the proof provided by this ministry, they will glorify God because of your obedient confession of the gospel of Christ, and for your generosity in sharing with them and with everyone."*
—2 Corinthians 9:13

SHORTLY AFTER BEGINNING TO work in fundraising, I had lunch with a seasoned fundraiser within Christian higher education. During our lunch, he asked me to share my thoughts on fundraising and how Christians should be engaged in generosity. I went on and on about how Christians should be giving their time, talent, and treasure as a way to serve the Lord as well as serve others. I thought I had waxed eloquently, talking about how we should be devoting our time to helping our local churches and other like-minded ministries, sharing our abilities with those whom we can serve, and financially supporting churches, pastors, missionaries, and ministries alike. As I went on and on over the course of about fifteen minutes, the gentleman I was having lunch with just sat back and listened with a smile on his face. Finally, as I finished talking, he leaned forward and told me something I will never forget. He said, "Nathan, you sure are passionate about engaging Christians to give their time, talent, and treasure. But you forgot the most important thing of all." I panicked; I had no idea what he was talking about. Sheepishly, I responded, "What is it?" He looked at me, smiled, and spoke with clarity, "Testimony, Nathan. Don't forget about your Christian testimony."

I left that lunch and realized I had been thinking about generosity all wrong. Generosity isn't about giving; it's about proclaiming and portraying the gospel of Jesus Christ. For Christians, generosity is more than just the way we give money, spend our time, and share our abilities with others. As we give, we get to be living examples of what Christ has done in our lives. Giving, above all else, is about the testimony of the gospel. Christian generosity has never been just about giving our time, talent, and treasure. When the gospel is the foundation for generosity, then giving is first and foremost about proclaiming and portraying the saving work of Christ. Because gospel generosity is rooted in the saving work of Christ, as we participate in the ministry of giving, we proclaim what Christ has done for us, and we portray it as we live according to the gospel. We proclaim the gospel through generosity because it's the gospel that calls us to live radically different from the world (Rom. 12:1–2). Also, it's through generosity that we portray the gospel to the world around us, because as we give, we exhibit the life transformation that only comes through the saving work of Jesus Christ (Col. 3:12–17). Because it's only by the power of the gospel that our hearts, minds, and pocketbooks are converted to be used for Christ, at His command, and for His glory.

As the apostle Paul nears the end of his teaching on giving, he tells the Corinthian church about how generosity proclaims and portrays the gospel.

> Because of the proof provided by this min-
> istry, they will glorify God because of your
> obedient confession of the gospel of Christ,

and for your generosity in sharing with them
and with everyone. (2 Cor. 9:13)

This is one of the most powerful statements we find in
the New Testament on the effects of giving. What does Paul
say happens when Christians are generous? People will glorify
God because of the confession of the gospel and the act of giving. Through generosity, Christians proclaim the gospel and
portray the gospel, which leads people to glorify God. Paul
didn't want the Corinthians, or us, to think that our own sat-
isfaction is the reason for giving; no, it's that generosity exalts
the risen Christ. The gift itself is not the focus of generosity,
but glorifying God through proclaiming and portraying the
gospel is.

How do we proclaim the gospel through generosity?
As the apostle Paul said, that by giving generously, the
Corinthian church showed their obedience to the confession
of their faith—the gospel of Jesus Christ. It was their obedient
confession that proclaimed their faith through generosity that
glorified God. But what exactly was their confession? Their
confession is found in the life, death, and resurrection of Jesus
(1 Cor. 15:3–4). The Corinthians aren't confessing their own

goodness in giving but are pointing everyone to the gospel of Jesus Christ. By their obedient confession of the gospel, the Corinthians proclaimed that generosity is all about the One who has saved them and sanctified them. Generosity is nothing but a vehicle to proclaim the goodness of God and the saving work of Jesus. As Christians, giving is always about proclaiming the work of God in one's life, because it's only by the gospel that we are able to give generously. The Corinthians weren't the focus of giving but pointed everyone to the good giver of all things—God (James 1:17). God is glorified when we give because we confess the gospel through generosity.

We give generously because of the gospel, and only because of the gospel. Without the gospel, we would not give humbly, selflessly, or with fidelity. Without the gospel, we wouldn't see generosity as an act of grace, leading us to cheerfulness that trusts in the Lord to provide, as we are equipped for every good work and value the needs of others more than our own. The act of giving portrays the gospel because it puts our money where our mouth is! It's one thing to confess the gospel and the saving work of Christ, but it's another to exhibit the life changes that accompany it. If we confess the gospel, then generosity should naturally follow. As we practice generosity, God is working through us, enabling us to give.

I said at the beginning of this book that gospel generosity is simply giving that is rooted in the saving work of Jesus Christ. It is the Christian's joyful awareness of what Christ has done for us and how we are privileged to participate in proclaiming that work through giving and advancing the gospel. Through this book, we've seen how generosity is rooted in the gospel, sprouts from the gospel, and bears fruit because of the gospel. Giving is not merely a virtue for the Christian life, but it is a cheerful disposition that springs forth from the good news of salvation in Jesus Christ. It is a sign of the radical reforming of the believer's head and heart to joyfully serve the Lord through the stewardship of their resources. Therefore, generosity for the Christian is not just about giving but is about proclaiming and portraying the saving work of God. Go, give generously, and glorify God!

# Notes

## Chapter 1

1. While it is a commonly held belief that famed reformer Martin Luther is the originator of this idea, there is no discernible source for this thought.

2. Madge Thornall Roberts, *The Star of Destiny: The Private Life of Sam and Margaret Houston* (Denton, TX: University of North Texas Press, 2001), 252. Though the narrative of the interaction between Houston and the pastor is likely to be exaggerated, Houston still later remarked that his pocketbook, too, had been baptized that day.

## Chapter 2

1. In Genesis 4, we find two brothers each making an offering to God. Abel offered God some of the "firstborn" of his flock, while Cain is said to bring only "some" of the land's produce. While Scripture doesn't say exactly why Cain's offering was not accepted, one reading could be that Abel brought his best—the first—while Cain did not. God accepted Abel's offering but rejected Cain's.

2. Laura Numeroff and Felicia Bond, illustrator, *If You Give a Moose a Muffin* (New York: HarperCollins, 1991).

3. This quick explanation does not do justice to all the processes that take place between your eyes receiving light and your brain registering images, but it is a start.

4. "When the eye is functioning normally, the light it perceives means illumination of benefit to the whole body." Leon Morris, *The Gospel according to Matthew,* The Pillar New Testament Commentary (Grand Rapids: Wm. B. Eerdmans Publishing Co.), 1992, 154.

5. Morris, *Matthew,* 154.

6. C. H. Spurgeon, *The Gospel of the Kingdom: A Popular Exposition of the Gospel According to Matthew* (London: Passmore and Alabaster, 1893), 64.

## Chapter 3

1. Samuel Johnson, "The Vision of Theodore, the Hermit of Teneriffe, Found in His Cell," *The Gentleman's Magazine,* vol. 18 (London: E. Cave, St. John's Gate, 1748), 160.

2. Jason DeRouchie, Oren R. Martin, and Andrew David Naselli, *40 Questions about Biblical Theology,* ed. Benjamin L. Merkle (Grand Rapids: Kregel Academic 2020), 246–48.

3. David A. Croteau, *Perspectives on Tithing: 4 Views* (Nashville: B&H Academic, 2011), 6.

4. Leon Morris, *The Gospel according to Matthew,* The Pillar New Testament Commentary (Grand Rapids: Wm. B. Eerdmans Publishing Co., 1992), 107.

5. Jason DeRouchie, *Understand and Apply the Old Testament: 12 Steps from Exegesis to Theology* (Phillipsburg, NJ: P&R Publishing, 2017), 439–59.

6. DeRouchie, *Understand and Apply the Old Testament*.

7. I am incredibly grateful for the scholarship and ministry of Jason DeRouchie. His work on the law has been formative to my life. He consistently shows how the law shows God's character, points people to Jesus, and teaches Christians how to live.

8. Thomas R. Schreiner, *40 Questions about Christians and Biblical Law* (Grand Rapids: Kregel Academic, 2010), 220.

9. John Webster, "Generosity," in *Christ Our Salvation: Expositions & Proclamations*, edited by Daniel Bush (Bellingham: Lexham Press, 2020), 127.

## Chapter 4

1. "There are about one hundred references to the kingdom in the Synoptic Gospels. There are two references in John (John 3:3, 5; 18:36), six in Acts, and eight in Paul's letters." Jeremy M. Kimble and Ched Spellman, *Invitation to Biblical Theology: Exploring the Shape, Storyline, and Themes of Scripture* (Grand Rapids: Kregel Academic, 2020), 278.

2. Patrick Schreiner, *The Kingdom of God and the Glory of the Cross* (Wheaton: Crossway, 2018), 18.

3. "It is not enough to indicate that one would like to be a follower of Jesus; to commit oneself to him means to commit oneself to a learning process. This is not meant to scare people or make them think that the way Jesus teaches is much harder than that of

the rabbis. Jesus affirms that he is *gentle and humble in heart*. This taking of a lowly place is noteworthy. Leaders and teachers have always tended to take a superior place, but Jesus has no need of such gimmicks. He left his place in heaven and on earth took the form of a slave (Phil. 2:7). *In heart* locates these qualities at the center of his being. It was not that he pretended to be humble and made a show of being lowly: he really was lowly, and that at the very center of all that he was." Leon Morris, *The Gospel according to Matthew*, The Pillar New Testament Commentary (Grand Rapids, MI; Leicester, England: W.B. Eerdmans; Inter-Varsity Press, 1992), 296–97.

4. "In addition to worship, the temple in Jerusalem, like nearly all temples in the ancient world, functioned as a depository for, and the administration of, vast amounts of wealth." James R. Edwards, *The Gospel according to Luke*, ed. D. A. Carson, The Pillar New Testament Commentary (Grand Rapids, MI; Cambridge, U.K.; Nottingham, England: William B. Eerdmans Publishing Company; Apollos, 2015), 587.

5. "The temple also functioned as a repository of individual wealth, in the belief that a sacred place was a safe place." Edwards, *The Gospel according to Luke*, 587.

6. Charles Haddon Spurgeon, "The Best Donation," *Metropolitan Tabernacle Pulpit, Sermons Preached and Revised*, vol. 37 (1891), 625.

7. "Mark is forcing his audience to reflect upon their personal commitment to Jesus and the kingdom here. They must ask themselves whether or not they have truly abandoned all and followed Jesus." Benjamin L. Gladd, *Handbook on the Gospels* (Grand Rapids: Baker Academic, 2021), 166.

8. "Running and kneeling are actions typical of a servant or slave, indicating the man's deference for Jesus and perhaps the urgency of his request." Mark L. Strauss, *Mark: Exegetical Commentary on the New Testament* (Grand Rapids: Zondervan Academic, 2014), 439.

9. It is highly contested as to whether or not this interaction ever happened. Regardless, the story that has been handed down for centuries still points us to an example of resolute faith in Christ.

## Chapter 5

1. For more on the ascension, see Patrick Schreiner's *The Ascension of Christ: Recovering a Neglected Doctrine* (Bellingham: Lexham Press, 2020).

2. "Through the word picture of sowing and harvesting, applied to financial giving in the church, Paul wants the Corinthians to grasp an important principle. Those who give grudgingly, and little will receive a tightfisted return. By contrast, generous, openhanded giving leads to lavish blessings in return. Of course those blessings come from God, for God as the ultimate giver is at the very heart of Paul's thought here." George Guthrie, *2 Corinthians*, Baker Exegetical Commentary (Grand Rapids: Baker Academic, 2015), 448.

3. Of course, this is simply an analogy for giving. Many conditions can hinder a harvest, even if you have sown all of your seed. This is not a promise of plenty, but a call to a posture of sowing.

4. I want to be clear. This passage is *not* teaching a form of the prosperity gospel, which wrongly teaches that God will always bless His people with health or wealth due to their obedience. Instead,

this is about a heart that goes above and beyond so that they may also serve their neighbor, which is a godly desire.

5. Charles Haddon Spurgeon, *The Salt-Cellars: Being a Collection of Proverbs Together with Homely Notes Thereon,* vol. 1 (1889; repr., London: Forgotten Books, 2015), 119.

6. William Eldridge Hatcher, *Along the Trail of the Friendly Years* (Sussex: Wentworth Press, 2019), 249.

7. Charles Haddon Spurgeon, *Lectures to My Students*, vol. 1 (Peabody, MA: Hendrickson Publishers, 2014), 8.

8. Thanks to Spurgeon scholar and pastor Dr. Ray Rhodes for this quote. Spurgeon, *An All-Round Ministry: Messages to Ministers and Students* (1900; repr., London: Counted Faithful, 2020), 173.

9. John Wesley, "On the Danger of Increasing Riches," ed. Thomas Jackson, Sermon 126 (1872 edition), http://www.word-sofwesley.com/libtext.cfm?srm=126.